C000111237

Device Onboarding
Complete Self-Assessment Guide

The guidance in this Self-Assessment is based on Device Onboarding best practices and standards in business process architecture, design and quality management. The guidance is also based on the professional judgment of the individual collaborators listed in the Acknowledgments.

Notice of rights

Trademarks

Table of Contents

About The Art of Service

The Art of Service, Business Process Architects since 2000, is dedicated to helping stakeholders achieve excellence.

Defining, designing, creating, and implementing a process to solve a stakeholders challenge or meet an objective is the most valuable role… In EVERY group, company, organization and department.

Unless you're talking a one-time, single-use project, there should be a process. Whether that process is managed and implemented by humans, AI, or a combination of the two, it needs to be designed by someone with a complex enough perspective to ask the right questions.

Someone capable of asking the right questions and step back and say, 'What are we really trying to accomplish here? And is there a different way to look at it?'

With The Art of Service's Standard Requirements Self-Assessments, we empower people who can do just that — whether their title is marketer, entrepreneur, manager, salesperson, consultant, Business Process Manager, executive assistant, IT Manager, CIO etc... —they are the people who rule the future. They are people who watch the process as it happens, and ask the right questions to make the process work better.

Contact us when you need any support with this Self-Assessment and any help with templates, blue-prints and examples of standard documents you might need:

http://theartofservice.com
service@theartofservice.com

Included Resources - how to access

Included with your purchase of the book is the Device

Onboarding Self-Assessment Spreadsheet Dashboard which contains all questions and Self-Assessment areas and auto-generates insights, graphs, and project RACI planning - all with examples to get you started right away.

How? Simply send an email to
access@theartofservice.com
with this books' title in the subject to get the Device Onboarding Self Assessment Tool right away.

You will receive the following contents with New and Updated specific criteria:

- The latest quick edition of the book in PDF

- The latest complete edition of the book in PDF, which criteria correspond to the criteria in...

- The Self-Assessment Excel Dashboard, and...

- Example pre-filled Self-Assessment Excel Dashboard to get familiar with results generation

- In-depth specific Checklists covering the topic

- Project management checklists and templates to assist with implementation

Purpose of this Self-Assessment

This Self-Assessment has been developed to improve understanding of the requirements and elements of Device Onboarding, based on best practices and standards in business process architecture, design and quality management.

It is designed to allow for a rapid Self-Assessment to determine how closely existing management practices and procedures correspond to the elements of the Self-Assessment.

The criteria of requirements and elements of Device Onboarding have been rephrased in the format of a Self-Assessment questionnaire, with a seven-criterion scoring system, as explained in this document.

In this format, even with limited background knowledge of Device Onboarding, a manager can quickly review existing operations to determine how they measure up to the standards. This in turn can serve as the starting point of a 'gap analysis' to identify management tools or system elements that might usefully be implemented in the organization to help improve overall performance.

How to use the Self-Assessment

On the following pages are a series of questions to identify to what extent your Device Onboarding initiative is complete in comparison to the requirements set in standards.

To facilitate answering the questions, there is a space in front of each question to enter a score on a scale of '1' to '5'.

1 Strongly Disagree

2 Disagree

3 Neutral

4 Agree

5 Strongly Agree

Read the question and rate it with the following in front of mind:

'In my belief,
the answer to this question is clearly defined'.

There are two ways in which you can choose to interpret this statement;
1. how aware are you that the answer to the question is clearly defined
2. for more in-depth analysis you can choose to gather evidence and confirm the answer to the question. This obviously will take more time, most Self-Assessment users opt for the first way to interpret the question and dig deeper later on based on the outcome of the overall Self-Assessment.

A score of '1' would mean that the answer is not clear at all, where a '5' would mean the answer is crystal clear and defined. Leave emtpy when the question is not applicable or you don't want to answer it, you can skip it without affecting your score. Write your score in the space provided.

After you have responded to all the appropriate statements in each section, compute your average score for that section, using the formula provided, and round to the nearest tenth. Then transfer to the corresponding spoke in the Device Onboarding Scorecard on the second next page of the Self-Assessment.

Your completed Device Onboarding Scorecard will give you a clear presentation of which Device Onboarding areas need attention.

Device Onboarding Scorecard Example

Example of how the finalized Scorecard can look like:

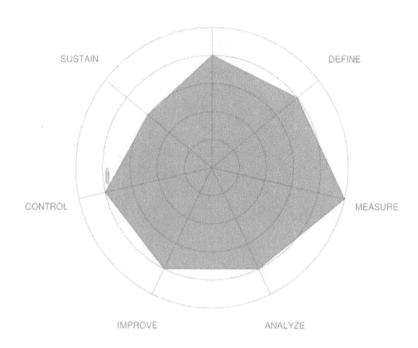

Device Onboarding Scorecard

Your Scores:

BEGINNING OF THE SELF-ASSESSMENT:

CRITERION #1: RECOGNIZE

INTENT: Be aware of the need for change. Recognize that there is an unfavorable variation, problem or symptom.

In my belief, the answer to this question is clearly defined:

5 Strongly Agree

4 Agree

3 Neutral

2 Disagree

1 Strongly Disagree

1. Are employees recognized for desired behaviors?
<--- Score

2. Who defines the rules in relation to any given issue?
<--- Score

3. Who else hopes to benefit from it?

<--- Score

4. As a sponsor, customer or management, how important is it to meet goals, objectives?
<--- Score

5. What does Device Onboarding success mean to the stakeholders?
<--- Score

6. Are there Device Onboarding problems defined?
<--- Score

7. What is the Device Onboarding problem definition? What do you need to resolve?
<--- Score

8. Who should resolve the Device Onboarding issues?
<--- Score

9. Why the need?
<--- Score

10. How do you assess your Device Onboarding workforce capability and capacity needs, including skills, competencies, and staffing levels?
<--- Score

11. Are there any specific expectations or concerns about the Device Onboarding team, Device Onboarding itself?
<--- Score

12. Will new equipment/products be required to facilitate Device Onboarding delivery, for example is new software needed?

<--- Score

13. Which issues are too important to ignore?
<--- Score

14. Who needs what information?
<--- Score

15. Whom do you really need or want to serve?
<--- Score

16. What should be considered when identifying available resources, constraints, and deadlines?
<--- Score

17. When a Device Onboarding manager recognizes a problem, what options are available?
<--- Score

18. Does the problem have ethical dimensions?
<--- Score

19. Are you dealing with any of the same issues today as yesterday? What can you do about this?
<--- Score

20. Will a response program recognize when a crisis occurs and provide some level of response?
<--- Score

21. What prevents you from making the changes you know will make you a more effective Device Onboarding leader?
<--- Score

22. What is the extent or complexity of the Device

Onboarding problem?
<--- Score

23. What are the expected benefits of Device Onboarding to the stakeholder?
<--- Score

24. Is the need for organizational change recognized?
<--- Score

25. Which needs are not included or involved?
<--- Score

26. What is the smallest subset of the problem you can usefully solve?
<--- Score

27. Do you need to avoid or amend any Device Onboarding activities?
<--- Score

28. Looking at each person individually – does every one have the qualities which are needed to work in this group?
<--- Score

29. Are employees recognized or rewarded for performance that demonstrates the highest levels of integrity?
<--- Score

30. What are the minority interests and what amount of minority interests can be recognized?
<--- Score

31. Did you miss any major Device Onboarding issues?

<--- Score

32. Why is this needed?
<--- Score

33. How are training requirements identified?
<--- Score

34. Are controls defined to recognize and contain problems?
<--- Score

35. For your Device Onboarding project, identify and describe the business environment, is there more than one layer to the business environment?
<--- Score

36. Are your goals realistic? Do you need to redefine your problem? Perhaps the problem has changed or maybe you have reached your goal and need to set a new one?
<--- Score

37. What needs to stay?
<--- Score

38. What are the clients issues and concerns?
<--- Score

39. How does it fit into your organizational needs and tasks?
<--- Score

40. Who needs to know about Device Onboarding?
<--- Score

41. What Device Onboarding coordination do you need?

<--- Score

42. Where do you need to exercise leadership?

<--- Score

43. Think about the people you identified for your Device Onboarding project and the project responsibilities you would assign to them, what kind of training do you think they would need to perform these responsibilities effectively?

<--- Score

44. Does Device Onboarding create potential expectations in other areas that need to be recognized and considered?

<--- Score

45. Who are your key stakeholders who need to sign off?

<--- Score

46. What else needs to be measured?

<--- Score

47. Where is training needed?

<--- Score

48. Who needs to know?

<--- Score

49. How much are sponsors, customers, partners, stakeholders involved in Device Onboarding? In other words, what are the risks, if Device Onboarding does not deliver successfully?

<--- Score

50. What problems are you facing and how do you consider Device Onboarding will circumvent those obstacles?
<--- Score

51. What training and capacity building actions are needed to implement proposed reforms?
<--- Score

52. What are your needs in relation to Device Onboarding skills, labor, equipment, and markets?
<--- Score

53. Are problem definition and motivation clearly presented?
<--- Score

54. What are the Device Onboarding resources needed?
<--- Score

55. What Device Onboarding problem should be solved?
<--- Score

56. What creative shifts do you need to take?
<--- Score

57. To what extent does each concerned units management team recognize Device Onboarding as an effective investment?
<--- Score

58. Do you need different information or graphics?

<--- Score

59. What is the recognized need?
<--- Score

60. Will it solve real problems?
<--- Score

61. How do you recognize an objection?
<--- Score

62. What extra resources will you need?
<--- Score

63. What resources or support might you need?
<--- Score

64. Consider your own Device Onboarding project, what types of organizational problems do you think might be causing or affecting your problem, based on the work done so far?
<--- Score

65. What Device Onboarding capabilities do you need?
<--- Score

66. How can auditing be a preventative security measure?
<--- Score

67. How do you identify subcontractor relationships?
<--- Score

68. What activities does the governance board

need to consider?
<--- Score

69. What situation(s) led to this Device Onboarding Self Assessment?
<--- Score

70. Is the quality assurance team identified?
<--- Score

71. How do you identify the kinds of information that you will need?
<--- Score

72. Are there recognized Device Onboarding problems?
<--- Score

73. Have you identified your Device Onboarding key performance indicators?
<--- Score

74. What information do users need?
<--- Score

75. What Device Onboarding events should you attend?
<--- Score

76. Is it clear when you think of the day ahead of you what activities and tasks you need to complete?
<--- Score

77. Do you know what you need to know about Device Onboarding?

<--- Score

78. What needs to be done?
<--- Score

79. Will Device Onboarding deliverables need to be tested and, if so, by whom?
<--- Score

80. What are the stakeholder objectives to be achieved with Device Onboarding?
<--- Score

81. Are losses recognized in a timely manner?
<--- Score

82. How many trainings, in total, are needed?
<--- Score

83. Who needs budgets?
<--- Score

84. Does your organization need more Device Onboarding education?
<--- Score

85. Is it needed?
<--- Score

86. To what extent would your organization benefit from being recognized as a award recipient?
<--- Score

87. What would happen if Device Onboarding weren't done?
<--- Score

88. How are you going to measure success?
<--- Score

89. Would you recognize a threat from the inside?
<--- Score

90. What vendors make products that address the Device Onboarding needs?
<--- Score

91. Are there any revenue recognition issues?
<--- Score

92. How do you recognize an Device Onboarding objection?
<--- Score

93. Which information does the Device Onboarding business case need to include?
<--- Score

94. How are the Device Onboarding's objectives aligned to the group's overall stakeholder strategy?
<--- Score

95. What do employees need in the short term?
<--- Score

96. What are the timeframes required to resolve each of the issues/problems?
<--- Score

97. What tools and technologies are needed for a custom Device Onboarding project?
<--- Score

98. How do you take a forward-looking perspective in identifying Device Onboarding research related to market response and models?
<--- Score

99. Do you recognize Device Onboarding achievements?
<--- Score

100. Can management personnel recognize the monetary benefit of Device Onboarding?
<--- Score

101. What do you need to start doing?
<--- Score

102. Are there regulatory / compliance issues?
<--- Score

Add up total points for this section:
_ _ _ _ _ = Total points for this section

Divided by: _ _ _ _ _ _ (number of statements answered) = _ _ _ _ _ _
Average score for this section

Transfer your score to the Device Onboarding Index at the beginning of the Self-Assessment.

CRITERION #2: DEFINE:

INTENT: Formulate the stakeholder problem. Define the problem, needs and objectives.

In my belief, the answer to this question is clearly defined:

5 Strongly Agree

4 Agree

3 Neutral

2 Disagree

1 Strongly Disagree

1. What is out of scope?
<--- Score

2. What specifically is the problem? Where does it occur? When does it occur? What is its extent?
<--- Score

3. Is there a completed SIPOC representation, describing the Suppliers, Inputs, Process, Outputs, and

Customers?

<--- Score

4. Has a high-level 'as is' process map been completed, verified and validated?

<--- Score

5. In what way can you redefine the criteria of choice clients have in your category in your favor?

<--- Score

6. How do you gather requirements?

<--- Score

7. Has a project plan, Gantt chart, or similar been developed/completed?

<--- Score

8. What is the scope?

<--- Score

9. What was the context?

<--- Score

10. Are audit criteria, scope, frequency and methods defined?

<--- Score

11. The political context: who holds power?

<--- Score

12. How will variation in the actual durations of each activity be dealt with to ensure that the expected Device Onboarding results are met?

<--- Score

13. Does the team have regular meetings?
<--- Score

14. What Device Onboarding services do you require?
<--- Score

15. How does the Device Onboarding manager ensure against scope creep?
<--- Score

16. How did the Device Onboarding manager receive input to the development of a Device Onboarding improvement plan and the estimated completion dates/times of each activity?
<--- Score

17. What customer feedback methods were used to solicit their input?
<--- Score

18. Has/have the customer(s) been identified?
<--- Score

19. Is Device Onboarding currently on schedule according to the plan?
<--- Score

20. What are the Device Onboarding tasks and definitions?
<--- Score

21. Has anyone else (internal or external to the group) attempted to solve this problem or a similar one before? If so, what knowledge can be leveraged from these previous efforts?

<--- Score

22. Is special Device Onboarding user knowledge required?
<--- Score

23. How have you defined all Device Onboarding requirements first?
<--- Score

24. What sort of initial information to gather?
<--- Score

25. How can the value of Device Onboarding be defined?
<--- Score

26. Who approved the Device Onboarding scope?
<--- Score

27. What scope to assess?
<--- Score

28. What is a worst-case scenario for losses?
<--- Score

29. How do you manage unclear Device Onboarding requirements?
<--- Score

30. Who is gathering information?
<--- Score

31. How often are the team meetings?
<--- Score

32. What key stakeholder process output measure(s) does Device Onboarding leverage and how?
<--- Score

33. What is the definition of Device Onboarding excellence?
<--- Score

34. What are the Roles and Responsibilities for each team member and its leadership? Where is this documented?
<--- Score

35. What is the context?
<--- Score

36. How do you build the right business case?
<--- Score

37. What is the definition of success?
<--- Score

38. How is the team tracking and documenting its work?
<--- Score

39. Is scope creep really all bad news?
<--- Score

40. Scope of sensitive information?
<--- Score

41. How would you define Device Onboarding leadership?
<--- Score

42. What defines best in class?

<--- Score

43. Are accountability and ownership for Device Onboarding clearly defined?

<--- Score

44. How would you define the culture at your organization, how susceptible is it to Device Onboarding changes?

<--- Score

45. Is there a critical path to deliver Device Onboarding results?

<--- Score

46. If substitutes have been appointed, have they been briefed on the Device Onboarding goals and received regular communications as to the progress to date?

<--- Score

47. What intelligence can you gather?

<--- Score

48. When are meeting minutes sent out? Who is on the distribution list?

<--- Score

49. Is there a clear Device Onboarding case definition?

<--- Score

50. What are the record-keeping requirements of Device Onboarding activities?

<--- Score

51. Are task requirements clearly defined?

<--- Score

52. What is out-of-scope initially?

<--- Score

53. What are the compelling stakeholder reasons for embarking on Device Onboarding?

<--- Score

54. Are there any constraints known that bear on the ability to perform Device Onboarding work? How is the team addressing them?

<--- Score

55. Has a team charter been developed and communicated?

<--- Score

56. What is in the scope and what is not in scope?

<--- Score

57. What is the scope of the Device Onboarding work?

<--- Score

58. How are consistent Device Onboarding definitions important?

<--- Score

59. What baselines are required to be defined and managed?

<--- Score

60. How do you think the partners involved in Device Onboarding would have defined success?

<--- Score

61. Has a Device Onboarding requirement not been met?

<--- Score

62. What are the dynamics of the communication plan?

<--- Score

63. Who defines (or who defined) the rules and roles?

<--- Score

64. What are the core elements of the Device Onboarding business case?

<--- Score

65. How do you gather the stories?

<--- Score

66. Does the scope remain the same?

<--- Score

67. Is there regularly 100% attendance at the team meetings? If not, have appointed substitutes attended to preserve cross-functionality and full representation?

<--- Score

68. Are the Device Onboarding requirements complete?

<--- Score

69. What gets examined?

<--- Score

70. Have all of the relationships been defined properly?
<--- Score

71. Is it clearly defined in and to your organization what you do?
<--- Score

72. What information do you gather?
<--- Score

73. Will a Device Onboarding production readiness review be required?
<--- Score

74. What is the scope of Device Onboarding?
<--- Score

75. Is the Device Onboarding scope manageable?
<--- Score

76. What critical content must be communicated – who, what, when, where, and how?
<--- Score

77. Has everyone on the team, including the team leaders, been properly trained?
<--- Score

78. Who is gathering Device Onboarding information?
<--- Score

79. Are different versions of process maps needed to account for the different types of inputs?
<--- Score

80. Is the Device Onboarding scope complete and appropriately sized?

<--- Score

81. Is the team adequately staffed with the desired cross-functionality? If not, what additional resources are available to the team?

<--- Score

82. When is/was the Device Onboarding start date?

<--- Score

83. What is the worst case scenario?

<--- Score

84. What are the boundaries of the scope? What is in bounds and what is not? What is the start point? What is the stop point?

<--- Score

85. Are approval levels defined for contracts and supplements to contracts?

<--- Score

86. Is Device Onboarding linked to key stakeholder goals and objectives?

<--- Score

87. What constraints exist that might impact the team?

<--- Score

88. Do you all define Device Onboarding in the same way?

<--- Score

89. When is the estimated completion date?
<--- Score

90. What are the requirements for audit information?
<--- Score

91. Who are the Device Onboarding improvement team members, including Management Leads and Coaches?
<--- Score

92. Do you have organizational privacy requirements?
<--- Score

93. How do you manage scope?
<--- Score

94. Are all requirements met?
<--- Score

95. What are the rough order estimates on cost savings/opportunities that Device Onboarding brings?
<--- Score

96. Are resources adequate for the scope?
<--- Score

97. How do you manage changes in Device Onboarding requirements?
<--- Score

98. Is Device Onboarding required?
<--- Score

99. Has the direction changed at all during the course of Device Onboarding? If so, when did it change and why?
<--- Score

100. Do the problem and goal statements meet the SMART criteria (specific, measurable, attainable, relevant, and time-bound)?
<--- Score

101. Why are you doing Device Onboarding and what is the scope?
<--- Score

102. Have all basic functions of Device Onboarding been defined?
<--- Score

103. What are the tasks and definitions?
<--- Score

104. Have the customer needs been translated into specific, measurable requirements? How?
<--- Score

105. How do you catch Device Onboarding definition inconsistencies?
<--- Score

106. What is the scope of the Device Onboarding effort?
<--- Score

107. Where can you gather more information?
<--- Score

108. Are required metrics defined, what are they?
<--- Score

109. What information should you gather?
<--- Score

110. How was the 'as is' process map developed, reviewed, verified and validated?
<--- Score

111. What are (control) requirements for Device Onboarding Information?
<--- Score

112. Is the current 'as is' process being followed? If not, what are the discrepancies?
<--- Score

113. Has your scope been defined?
<--- Score

114. Are there different segments of customers?
<--- Score

115. What scope do you want your strategy to cover?
<--- Score

116. Is there any additional Device Onboarding definition of success?
<--- Score

117. How will the Device Onboarding team and the group measure complete success of Device Onboarding?
<--- Score

118. How do you gather Device Onboarding requirements?
<--- Score

119. How do you keep key subject matter experts in the loop?
<--- Score

120. Is the scope of Device Onboarding defined?
<--- Score

121. What system do you use for gathering Device Onboarding information?
<--- Score

122. Are roles and responsibilities formally defined?
<--- Score

123. What would be the goal or target for a Device Onboarding's improvement team?
<--- Score

124. Has the improvement team collected the 'voice of the customer' (obtained feedback – qualitative and quantitative)?
<--- Score

125. Do you have a Device Onboarding success story or case study ready to tell and share?
<--- Score

126. What are the Device Onboarding use cases?
<--- Score

127. Has the Device Onboarding work been fairly and/or equitably divided and delegated among team

members who are qualified and capable to perform the work? Has everyone contributed?
<--- Score

128. What sources do you use to gather information for a Device Onboarding study?
<--- Score

129. What happens if Device Onboarding's scope changes?
<--- Score

130. Is the improvement team aware of the different versions of a process: what they think it is vs. what it actually is vs. what it should be vs. what it could be?
<--- Score

Add up total points for this section:
_ _ _ _ _ = Total points for this section

Divided by: _ _ _ _ _ _ (number of statements answered) = _ _ _ _ _ _ Average score for this section

Transfer your score to the Device Onboarding Index at the beginning of the Self-Assessment.

CRITERION #3: MEASURE:

INTENT: Gather the correct data. Measure the current performance and evolution of the situation.

In my belief, the answer to this question is clearly defined:

5 Strongly Agree

4 Agree

3 Neutral

2 Disagree

1 Strongly Disagree

1. Are you able to realize any cost savings?
<--- Score

2. How can you reduce costs?
<--- Score

3. What is the root cause(s) of the problem?
<--- Score

4. When should you bother with diagrams?
<--- Score

5. What causes mismanagement?
<--- Score

6. What causes innovation to fail or succeed in your organization?
<--- Score

7. What would it cost to replace your technology?
<--- Score

8. Are actual costs in line with budgeted costs?
<--- Score

9. How are costs allocated?
<--- Score

10. What are the strategic priorities for this year?
<--- Score

11. How will measures be used to manage and adapt?
<--- Score

12. What is the total cost related to deploying Device Onboarding, including any consulting or professional services?
<--- Score

13. How will you measure success?
<--- Score

14. Does the Device Onboarding task fit the client's priorities?
<--- Score

15. What disadvantage does this cause for the user?
<--- Score

16. How can you measure the performance?
<--- Score

17. What would be a real cause for concern?
<--- Score

18. What are the costs of delaying Device Onboarding action?
<--- Score

19. When are costs are incurred?
<--- Score

20. How sensitive must the Device Onboarding strategy be to cost?
<--- Score

21. What are your primary costs, revenues, assets?
<--- Score

22. Are there competing Device Onboarding priorities?
<--- Score

23. What is the cost of rework?
<--- Score

24. Does a Device Onboarding quantification method exist?
<--- Score

25. What does verifying compliance entail?

<--- Score

26. Is it possible to estimate the impact of unanticipated complexity such as wrong or failed assumptions, feedback, etcetera on proposed reforms?
<--- Score

27. What are the estimated costs of proposed changes?
<--- Score

28. Have you made assumptions about the shape of the future, particularly its impact on your customers and competitors?
<--- Score

29. How do you verify the authenticity of the data and information used?
<--- Score

30. Are you taking your company in the direction of better and revenue or cheaper and cost?
<--- Score

31. How are measurements made?
<--- Score

32. Are there any easy-to-implement alternatives to Device Onboarding? Sometimes other solutions are available that do not require the cost implications of a full-blown project?
<--- Score

33. Where can you go to verify the info?
<--- Score

34. What measurements are possible, practicable and meaningful?
<--- Score

35. What tests verify requirements?
<--- Score

36. What is your decision requirements diagram?
<--- Score

37. Do you verify that corrective actions were taken?
<--- Score

38. What is your Device Onboarding quality cost segregation study?
<--- Score

39. Is the cost worth the Device Onboarding effort ?
<--- Score

40. Do you effectively measure and reward individual and team performance?
<--- Score

41. What are the Device Onboarding investment costs?
<--- Score

42. What details are required of the Device Onboarding cost structure?
<--- Score

43. What is measured? Why?
<--- Score

44. Among the Device Onboarding product and service cost to be estimated, which is considered hardest to estimate?
<--- Score

45. What are the types and number of measures to use?
<--- Score

46. Are there measurements based on task performance?
<--- Score

47. Why do you expend time and effort to implement measurement, for whom?
<--- Score

48. How do you measure lifecycle phases?
<--- Score

49. How do you verify Device Onboarding completeness and accuracy?
<--- Score

50. Are you aware of what could cause a problem?
<--- Score

51. Is there an opportunity to verify requirements?
<--- Score

52. What is the total fixed cost?
<--- Score

53. What are your customers expectations and measures?

<--- Score

54. Why a Device Onboarding focus?
<--- Score

55. Are indirect costs charged to the Device Onboarding program?
<--- Score

56. How is the value delivered by Device Onboarding being measured?
<--- Score

57. What is the cause of any Device Onboarding gaps?
<--- Score

58. Who is involved in verifying compliance?
<--- Score

59. Which Device Onboarding impacts are significant?
<--- Score

60. Do you have an issue in getting priority?
<--- Score

61. Which measures and indicators matter?
<--- Score

62. How do you verify and develop ideas and innovations?
<--- Score

63. How will you measure your Device Onboarding effectiveness?
<--- Score

64. How do you verify if Device Onboarding is built right?

<--- Score

65. How do you verify performance?

<--- Score

66. How frequently do you track Device Onboarding measures?

<--- Score

67. What drives O&M cost?

<--- Score

68. How much does it cost?

<--- Score

69. What are you verifying?

<--- Score

70. How can you manage cost down?

<--- Score

71. When a disaster occurs, who gets priority?

<--- Score

72. What harm might be caused?

<--- Score

73. Are missed Device Onboarding opportunities costing your organization money?

<--- Score

74. How can a Device Onboarding test verify your ideas or assumptions?

<--- Score

75. What could cause delays in the schedule?
<--- Score

76. At what cost?
<--- Score

77. Do you have any cost Device Onboarding limitation requirements?
<--- Score

78. Where is the cost?
<--- Score

79. What are the Device Onboarding key cost drivers?
<--- Score

80. How do you verify the Device Onboarding requirements quality?
<--- Score

81. What are the operational costs after Device Onboarding deployment?
<--- Score

82. What is an unallowable cost?
<--- Score

83. What does your operating model cost?
<--- Score

84. How do you prevent mis-estimating cost?
<--- Score

85. How do you aggregate measures across priorities?

<--- Score

86. Does management have the right priorities among projects?
<--- Score

87. How can you reduce the costs of obtaining inputs?
<--- Score

88. What potential environmental factors impact the Device Onboarding effort?
<--- Score

89. Where is it measured?
<--- Score

90. How will your organization measure success?
<--- Score

91. What methods are feasible and acceptable to estimate the impact of reforms?
<--- Score

92. What does a Test Case verify?
<--- Score

93. What measurements are being captured?
<--- Score

94. How will success or failure be measured?
<--- Score

95. What happens if cost savings do not materialize?
<--- Score

96. Are the Device Onboarding benefits worth its

costs?
<--- Score

97. What are hidden Device Onboarding quality costs?
<--- Score

98. How long to keep data and how to manage retention costs?
<--- Score

99. Are Device Onboarding vulnerabilities categorized and prioritized?
<--- Score

100. How do you measure efficient delivery of Device Onboarding services?
<--- Score

101. What are the current costs of the Device Onboarding process?
<--- Score

102. What can be used to verify compliance?
<--- Score

103. Are supply costs steady or fluctuating?
<--- Score

104. What are your key Device Onboarding organizational performance measures, including key short and longer-term financial measures?
<--- Score

105. What do people want to verify?
<--- Score

106. How to cause the change?

<--- Score

107. What could cause you to change course?

<--- Score

108. What are the costs of reform?

<--- Score

109. Do you have a flow diagram of what happens?

<--- Score

110. Why do the measurements/indicators matter?

<--- Score

111. How will costs be allocated?

<--- Score

112. How can you measure Device Onboarding in a systematic way?

<--- Score

113. What relevant entities could be measured?

<--- Score

114. How do you measure success?

<--- Score

115. Have design-to-cost goals been established?

<--- Score

116. What causes extra work or rework?

<--- Score

117. What are the uncertainties surrounding estimates of impact?

<--- Score

118. Are the measurements objective?
<--- Score

119. Are the units of measure consistent?
<--- Score

120. What causes investor action?
<--- Score

121. Do the benefits outweigh the costs?
<--- Score

122. What are your operating costs?
<--- Score

123. Which costs should be taken into account?
<--- Score

124. What evidence is there and what is measured?
<--- Score

125. How do you measure variability?
<--- Score

126. Was a business case (cost/benefit) developed?
<--- Score

127. Did you tackle the cause or the symptom?
<--- Score

128. How do you verify your resources?
<--- Score

129. How are you verifying it?

<--- Score

130. Is the solution cost-effective?
<--- Score

131. Who should receive measurement reports?
<--- Score

132. How frequently do you verify your Device Onboarding strategy?
<--- Score

133. How will effects be measured?
<--- Score

134. What are the costs?
<--- Score

135. How do you verify and validate the Device Onboarding data?
<--- Score

136. How is progress measured?
<--- Score

137. What users will be impacted?
<--- Score

Add up total points for this section:
_ _ _ _ _ = Total points for this section

Divided by: _ _ _ _ _ _ (number of statements answered) = _ _ _ _ _ _
Average score for this section

Transfer your score to the Device

Onboarding Index at the beginning of
the Self-Assessment.

CRITERION #4: ANALYZE:

INTENT: Analyze causes, assumptions and hypotheses.

In my belief, the answer to this question is clearly defined:

5 Strongly Agree

4 Agree

3 Neutral

2 Disagree

1 Strongly Disagree

1. Who gets your output?
<--- Score

2. Should you invest in industry-recognized qualifications?
<--- Score

3. Do quality systems drive continuous improvement?
<--- Score

4. Think about the functions involved in your Device Onboarding project, what processes flow from these functions?

<--- Score

5. Identify an operational issue in your organization, for example, could a particular task be done more quickly or more efficiently by Device Onboarding?

<--- Score

6. What Device Onboarding data should be managed?

<--- Score

7. How will the Device Onboarding data be captured?

<--- Score

8. How many input/output points does it require?

<--- Score

9. What are your best practices for minimizing Device Onboarding project risk, while demonstrating incremental value and quick wins throughout the Device Onboarding project lifecycle?

<--- Score

10. What were the crucial 'moments of truth' on the process map?

<--- Score

11. How will corresponding data be collected?

<--- Score

12. What kind of crime could a potential new hire

have committed that would not only not disqualify him/her from being hired by your organization, but would actually indicate that he/she might be a particularly good fit?
<--- Score

13. How do you promote understanding that opportunity for improvement is not criticism of the status quo, or the people who created the status quo?
<--- Score

14. Do staff qualifications match your project?
<--- Score

15. What are your current levels and trends in key Device Onboarding measures or indicators of product and process performance that are important to and directly serve your customers?
<--- Score

16. How difficult is it to qualify what Device Onboarding ROI is?
<--- Score

17. What quality tools were used to get through the analyze phase?
<--- Score

18. What, related to, Device Onboarding processes does your organization outsource?
<--- Score

19. How do you define collaboration and team output?
<--- Score

20. Was a cause-and-effect diagram used to explore the different types of causes (or sources of variation)?
<--- Score

21. Who is involved in the management review process?
<--- Score

22. Were there any improvement opportunities identified from the process analysis?
<--- Score

23. Was a detailed process map created to amplify critical steps of the 'as is' stakeholder process?
<--- Score

24. Where can you get qualified talent today?
<--- Score

25. Who qualifies to gain access to data?
<--- Score

26. What controls do you have in place to protect data?
<--- Score

27. Is the performance gap determined?
<--- Score

28. Do your contracts/agreements contain data security obligations?
<--- Score

29. Who is involved with workflow mapping?
<--- Score

30. Have the problem and goal statements been updated to reflect the additional knowledge gained from the analyze phase?
<--- Score

31. What qualifications and skills do you need?
<--- Score

32. Do you, as a leader, bounce back quickly from setbacks?
<--- Score

33. What do you need to qualify?
<--- Score

34. What are your key performance measures or indicators and in-process measures for the control and improvement of your Device Onboarding processes?
<--- Score

35. Are all staff in core Device Onboarding subjects Highly Qualified?
<--- Score

36. What does the data say about the performance of the stakeholder process?
<--- Score

37. Do several people in different organizational units assist with the Device Onboarding process?
<--- Score

38. What Device Onboarding data should be collected?
<--- Score

39. An organizationally feasible system request is one that considers the mission, goals and objectives of the organization, key questions are: is the Device Onboarding solution request practical and will it solve a problem or take advantage of an opportunity to achieve company goals?
<--- Score

40. What is your organizations system for selecting qualified vendors?
<--- Score

41. How has the Device Onboarding data been gathered?
<--- Score

42. What qualifications are necessary?
<--- Score

43. What conclusions were drawn from the team's data collection and analysis? How did the team reach these conclusions?
<--- Score

44. What is the oversight process?
<--- Score

45. A compounding model resolution with available relevant data can often provide insight towards a solution methodology; which Device Onboarding models, tools and techniques are necessary?
<--- Score

46. Who owns what data?
<--- Score

47. Did any value-added analysis or 'lean thinking' take place to identify some of the gaps shown on the 'as is' process map?
<--- Score

48. Is the required Device Onboarding data gathered?
<--- Score

49. Have any additional benefits been identified that will result from closing all or most of the gaps?
<--- Score

50. What tools were used to narrow the list of possible causes?
<--- Score

51. What are the processes for audit reporting and management?
<--- Score

52. Are your outputs consistent?
<--- Score

53. What other jobs or tasks affect the performance of the steps in the Device Onboarding process?
<--- Score

54. Are Device Onboarding changes recognized early enough to be approved through the regular process?
<--- Score

55. Can you add value to the current Device Onboarding decision-making process (largely qualitative) by incorporating uncertainty modeling (more quantitative)?

<--- Score

56. How is Device Onboarding data gathered?
<--- Score

57. What Device Onboarding data will be collected?
<--- Score

58. What is the cost of poor quality as supported by the team's analysis?
<--- Score

59. What are the Device Onboarding business drivers?
<--- Score

60. Is there a strict change management process?
<--- Score

61. Is the suppliers process defined and controlled?
<--- Score

62. How do you measure the operational performance of your key work systems and processes, including productivity, cycle time, and other appropriate measures of process effectiveness, efficiency, and innovation?
<--- Score

63. Is the final output clearly identified?
<--- Score

64. Where is Device Onboarding data gathered?
<--- Score

65. Which Device Onboarding data should be retained?

<--- Score

66. How is the Device Onboarding Value Stream Mapping managed?
<--- Score

67. How is the data gathered?
<--- Score

68. How does the organization define, manage, and improve its Device Onboarding processes?
<--- Score

69. What process should you select for improvement?
<--- Score

70. Are you missing Device Onboarding opportunities?
<--- Score

71. What are the necessary qualifications?
<--- Score

72. How can risk management be tied procedurally to process elements?
<--- Score

73. How do you ensure that the Device Onboarding opportunity is realistic?
<--- Score

74. Do you have the authority to produce the output?
<--- Score

75. How do you use Device Onboarding data and

information to support organizational decision making and innovation?
<--- Score

76. What output to create?
<--- Score

77. What is the Device Onboarding Driver?
<--- Score

78. What training and qualifications will you need?
<--- Score

79. Where is the data coming from to measure compliance?
<--- Score

80. What are the revised rough estimates of the financial savings/opportunity for Device Onboarding improvements?
<--- Score

81. What methods do you use to gather Device Onboarding data?
<--- Score

82. Did any additional data need to be collected?
<--- Score

83. What Device Onboarding metrics are outputs of the process?
<--- Score

84. What is the complexity of the output produced?
<--- Score

85. What qualifies as competition?
<--- Score

86. What other organizational variables, such as reward systems or communication systems, affect the performance of this Device Onboarding process?
<--- Score

87. What qualifications are needed?
<--- Score

88. Is data and process analysis, root cause analysis and quantifying the gap/opportunity in place?
<--- Score

89. How do your work systems and key work processes relate to and capitalize on your core competencies?
<--- Score

90. What will drive Device Onboarding change?
<--- Score

91. What process improvements will be needed?
<--- Score

92. When should a process be art not science?
<--- Score

93. What data is gathered?
<--- Score

94. Do you understand your management processes today?

<--- Score

95. What is your organizations process which leads to recognition of value generation?
<--- Score

96. Record-keeping requirements flow from the records needed as inputs, outputs, controls and for transformation of a Device Onboarding process, are the records needed as inputs to the Device Onboarding process available?
<--- Score

97. What are your outputs?
<--- Score

98. What information qualified as important?
<--- Score

99. Are gaps between current performance and the goal performance identified?
<--- Score

100. How will the change process be managed?
<--- Score

101. What qualifications do Device Onboarding leaders need?
<--- Score

102. Is there an established change management process?
<--- Score

103. How are outputs preserved and protected?
<--- Score

104. Have you defined which data is gathered how?

<--- Score

105. What systems/processes must you excel at?

<--- Score

106. Is the Device Onboarding process severely broken such that a re-design is necessary?

<--- Score

107. Think about some of the processes you undertake within your organization, which do you own?

<--- Score

108. Do your employees have the opportunity to do what they do best everyday?

<--- Score

109. Is pre-qualification of suppliers carried out?

<--- Score

110. Were Pareto charts (or similar) used to portray the 'heavy hitters' (or key sources of variation)?

<--- Score

111. How often will data be collected for measures?

<--- Score

112. Were any designed experiments used to generate additional insight into the data analysis?

<--- Score

113. What internal processes need improvement?
<--- Score

114. What did the team gain from developing a sub-process map?
<--- Score

115. What were the financial benefits resulting from any 'ground fruit or low-hanging fruit' (quick fixes)?
<--- Score

116. How is the way you as the leader think and process information affecting your organizational culture?
<--- Score

117. How was the detailed process map generated, verified, and validated?
<--- Score

118. Is the gap/opportunity displayed and communicated in financial terms?
<--- Score

119. Do your leaders quickly bounce back from setbacks?
<--- Score

120. Who will facilitate the team and process?
<--- Score

121. How much data can be collected in the given timeframe?
<--- Score

122. What is the Value Stream Mapping?

<--- Score

123. Who will gather what data?
<--- Score

124. What Device Onboarding data do you gather or use now?
<--- Score

125. What is the output?
<--- Score

126. What are the personnel training and qualifications required?
<--- Score

127. What types of data do your Device Onboarding indicators require?
<--- Score

128. How do you identify specific Device Onboarding investment opportunities and emerging trends?
<--- Score

129. Has data output been validated?
<--- Score

130. What tools were used to generate the list of possible causes?
<--- Score

131. Is there any way to speed up the process?
<--- Score

132. How do you implement and manage your work processes to ensure that they meet design

requirements?
<--- Score

133. What data do you need to collect?
<--- Score

134. How will the data be checked for quality?
<--- Score

Add up total points for this section:
_ _ _ _ _ = Total points for this section

Divided by: _ _ _ _ _ _ (number of
statements answered) = _ _ _ _ _ _
Average score for this section

Transfer your score to the Device
Onboarding Index at the beginning of
the Self-Assessment.

CRITERION #5: IMPROVE:

INTENT: Develop a practical solution. Innovate, establish and test the solution and to measure the results.

In my belief, the answer to this question is clearly defined:

5 Strongly Agree

4 Agree

3 Neutral

2 Disagree

1 Strongly Disagree

1. How can you improve Device Onboarding?
<--- Score

2. How will you know that you have improved?
<--- Score

3. How can the phases of Device Onboarding development be identified?
<--- Score

4. Who do you report Device Onboarding results to?
<--- Score

5. What were the criteria for evaluating a Device Onboarding pilot?
<--- Score

6. What lessons, if any, from a pilot were incorporated into the design of the full-scale solution?
<--- Score

7. What criteria will you use to assess your Device Onboarding risks?
<--- Score

8. Have you achieved Device Onboarding improvements?
<--- Score

9. What tools were used to evaluate the potential solutions?
<--- Score

10. How do you improve your likelihood of success ?
<--- Score

11. What does the 'should be' process map/design look like?
<--- Score

12. Is supporting Device Onboarding documentation required?
<--- Score

13. How will you know that a change is an improvement?
<--- Score

14. Are the most efficient solutions problem-specific?
<--- Score

15. Who controls the risk?
<--- Score

16. How is continuous improvement applied to risk management?
<--- Score

17. For decision problems, how do you develop a decision statement?
<--- Score

18. What to do with the results or outcomes of measurements?
<--- Score

19. To what extent does management recognize Device Onboarding as a tool to increase the results?
<--- Score

20. What Device Onboarding improvements can be made?
<--- Score

21. What can you do to improve?
<--- Score

22. What were the underlying assumptions on the cost-benefit analysis?
<--- Score

23. How will you measure the results?
<--- Score

24. Are procedures documented for managing Device Onboarding risks?
<--- Score

25. What assumptions are made about the solution and approach?
<--- Score

26. Is the measure of success for Device Onboarding understandable to a variety of people?
<--- Score

27. Can you identify any significant risks or exposures to Device Onboarding third- parties (vendors, service providers, alliance partners etc) that concern you?
<--- Score

28. Who manages Device Onboarding risk?
<--- Score

29. How do you mitigate Device Onboarding risk?
<--- Score

30. What attendant changes will need to be made to ensure that the solution is successful?
<--- Score

31. Who should make the Device Onboarding decisions?
<--- Score

32. How risky is your organization?

<--- Score

33. If you could go back in time five years, what decision would you make differently? What is your best guess as to what decision you're making today you might regret five years from now?

<--- Score

34. Is any Device Onboarding documentation required?

<--- Score

35. What are the concrete Device Onboarding results?

<--- Score

36. How do you go about comparing Device Onboarding approaches/solutions?

<--- Score

37. When you map the key players in your own work and the types/domains of relationships with them, which relationships do you find easy and which challenging, and why?

<--- Score

38. What is the Device Onboarding's sustainability risk?

<--- Score

39. What are the implications of the one critical Device Onboarding decision 10 minutes, 10 months, and 10 years from now?

<--- Score

40. Was a pilot designed for the proposed solution(s)?
<--- Score

41. What improvements have been achieved?
<--- Score

42. How can you improve performance?
<--- Score

43. How will you know when its improved?
<--- Score

44. How do you improve Device Onboarding service perception, and satisfaction?
<--- Score

45. What area needs the greatest improvement?
<--- Score

46. Is there any other Device Onboarding solution?
<--- Score

47. What are the expected Device Onboarding results?
<--- Score

48. What are the affordable Device Onboarding risks?
<--- Score

49. Do you have the optimal project management team structure?
<--- Score

50. Who are the Device Onboarding decision-makers?
<--- Score

51. Is the scope clearly documented?
<--- Score

52. What risks do you need to manage?
<--- Score

53. Device Onboarding risk decisions: whose call Is It?
<--- Score

54. How can skill-level changes improve Device Onboarding?
<--- Score

55. Were any criteria developed to assist the team in testing and evaluating potential solutions?
<--- Score

56. How do you measure improved Device Onboarding service perception, and satisfaction?
<--- Score

57. Does the goal represent a desired result that can be measured?
<--- Score

58. Is risk periodically assessed?
<--- Score

59. How do you improve productivity?
<--- Score

60. How do you manage and improve your Device Onboarding work systems to deliver customer value and achieve organizational success and sustainability?
<--- Score

61. How do you define the solutions' scope?
<--- Score

62. How are Device Onboarding risks managed?
<--- Score

63. What should a proof of concept or pilot accomplish?
<--- Score

64. How can you better manage risk?
<--- Score

65. What are your current levels and trends in key measures or indicators of workforce and leader development?
<--- Score

66. Who will be using the results of the measurement activities?
<--- Score

67. What went well, what should change, what can improve?
<--- Score

68. How does your organization evaluate strategic Device Onboarding success?
<--- Score

69. How do you deal with Device Onboarding risk?
<--- Score

70. What do you want to improve?
<--- Score

71. Are the risks fully understood, reasonable and manageable?
<--- Score

72. Where do you need Device Onboarding improvement?
<--- Score

73. At what point will vulnerability assessments be performed once Device Onboarding is put into production (e.g., ongoing Risk Management after implementation)?
<--- Score

74. Who manages supplier risk management in your organization?
<--- Score

75. What practices helps your organization to develop its capacity to recognize patterns?
<--- Score

76. What is Device Onboarding risk?
<--- Score

77. Is the Device Onboarding risk managed?
<--- Score

78. Can you integrate quality management and risk management?
<--- Score

79. Who controls key decisions that will be made?
<--- Score

80. Do you combine technical expertise with

business knowledge and Device Onboarding Key topics include lifecycles, development approaches, requirements and how to make a business case?
<--- Score

81. Is the solution technically practical?
<--- Score

82. Who are the people involved in developing and implementing Device Onboarding?
<--- Score

83. Was a Device Onboarding charter developed?
<--- Score

84. How will you recognize and celebrate results?
<--- Score

85. Can the solution be designed and implemented within an acceptable time period?
<--- Score

86. Would you develop a Device Onboarding Communication Strategy?
<--- Score

87. Do you cover the five essential competencies: Communication, Collaboration,Innovation, Adaptability, and Leadership that improve an organizations ability to leverage the new Device Onboarding in a volatile global economy?
<--- Score

88. What communications are necessary to support the implementation of the solution?
<--- Score

89. Risk events: what are the things that could go wrong?
<--- Score

90. Is the Device Onboarding documentation thorough?
<--- Score

91. Are risk triggers captured?
<--- Score

92. Do vendor agreements bring new compliance risk ?
<--- Score

93. What is the magnitude of the improvements?
<--- Score

94. Where do the Device Onboarding decisions reside?
<--- Score

95. Which Device Onboarding solution is appropriate?
<--- Score

96. What tools do you use once you have decided on a Device Onboarding strategy and more importantly how do you choose?
<--- Score

97. What is the team's contingency plan for potential problems occurring in implementation?
<--- Score

98. Who will be responsible for making the decisions to include or exclude requested changes once Device Onboarding is underway?
<--- Score

99. What is the risk?
<--- Score

100. What tools were used to tap into the creativity and encourage 'outside the box' thinking?
<--- Score

101. Who will be responsible for documenting the Device Onboarding requirements in detail?
<--- Score

102. What is Device Onboarding's impact on utilizing the best solution(s)?
<--- Score

103. Who are the key stakeholders for the Device Onboarding evaluation?
<--- Score

104. Are you assessing Device Onboarding and risk?
<--- Score

105. What is the implementation plan?
<--- Score

106. Are the key business and technology risks being managed?
<--- Score

107. For estimation problems, how do you develop an estimation statement?

<--- Score

108. How do you measure risk?
<--- Score

109. Risk Identification: What are the possible risk events your organization faces in relation to Device Onboarding?
<--- Score

110. What are the Device Onboarding security risks?
<--- Score

111. Are events managed to resolution?
<--- Score

112. How do you decide how much to remunerate an employee?
<--- Score

113. In the past few months, what is the smallest change you have made that has had the biggest positive result? What was it about that small change that produced the large return?
<--- Score

114. What current systems have to be understood and/or changed?
<--- Score

115. Are decisions made in a timely manner?
<--- Score

116. Risk factors: what are the characteristics of Device Onboarding that make it risky?
<--- Score

117. Does a good decision guarantee a good outcome?
<--- Score

118. How significant is the improvement in the eyes of the end user?
<--- Score

119. Who makes the Device Onboarding decisions in your organization?
<--- Score

120. Which of the recognised risks out of all risks can be most likely transferred?
<--- Score

121. How do the Device Onboarding results compare with the performance of your competitors and other organizations with similar offerings?
<--- Score

122. Do you need to do a usability evaluation?
<--- Score

123. What error proofing will be done to address some of the discrepancies observed in the 'as is' process?
<--- Score

124. How do you link measurement and risk?
<--- Score

125. What resources are required for the improvement efforts?
<--- Score

126. Have you identified breakpoints and/or risk tolerances that will trigger broad consideration of a potential need for intervention or modification of strategy?

<--- Score

127. Do those selected for the Device Onboarding team have a good general understanding of what Device Onboarding is all about?

<--- Score

128. What needs improvement? Why?

<--- Score

129. What tools were most useful during the improve phase?

<--- Score

130. Why improve in the first place?

<--- Score

Add up total points for this section:
_ _ _ _ _ = Total points for this section

Divided by: _ _ _ _ _ _ (number of statements answered) = _ _ _ _ _ _
Average score for this section

Transfer your score to the Device Onboarding Index at the beginning of the Self-Assessment.

CRITERION #6: CONTROL:

INTENT: Implement the practical solution. Maintain the performance and correct possible complications.

In my belief, the answer to this question is clearly defined:

5 Strongly Agree

4 Agree

3 Neutral

2 Disagree

1 Strongly Disagree

1. Has the Device Onboarding value of standards been quantified?
<--- Score

2. Will existing staff require re-training, for example, to learn new business processes?
<--- Score

3. What is the standard for acceptable Device

Onboarding performance?
<--- Score

4. Can support from partners be adjusted?
<--- Score

5. What are customers monitoring?
<--- Score

6. How will you measure your QA plan's effectiveness?
<--- Score

7. How widespread is its use?
<--- Score

8. What adjustments to the strategies are needed?
<--- Score

9. What are the critical parameters to watch?
<--- Score

10. Is there a transfer of ownership and knowledge to process owner and process team tasked with the responsibilities.
<--- Score

11. What is the recommended frequency of auditing?
<--- Score

12. Does the response plan contain a definite closed loop continual improvement scheme (e.g., plan-do-check-act)?
<--- Score

13. How do you plan on providing proper recognition

and disclosure of supporting companies?
<--- Score

14. Will your goals reflect your program budget?
<--- Score

15. Is new knowledge gained imbedded in the response plan?
<--- Score

16. Are operating procedures consistent?
<--- Score

17. Does the Device Onboarding performance meet the customer's requirements?
<--- Score

18. Who is the Device Onboarding process owner?
<--- Score

19. How do you plan for the cost of succession?
<--- Score

20. Act/Adjust: What Do you Need to Do Differently?
<--- Score

21. What are your results for key measures or indicators of the accomplishment of your Device Onboarding strategy and action plans, including building and strengthening core competencies?
<--- Score

22. How is change control managed?
<--- Score

23. Is knowledge gained on process shared and

institutionalized?
<--- Score

24. What Device Onboarding standards are applicable?
<--- Score

25. Is there an action plan in case of emergencies?
<--- Score

26. What quality tools were useful in the control phase?
<--- Score

27. Is the Device Onboarding test/monitoring cost justified?
<--- Score

28. How do your controls stack up?
<--- Score

29. Is reporting being used or needed?
<--- Score

30. Are new process steps, standards, and documentation ingrained into normal operations?
<--- Score

31. Does job training on the documented procedures need to be part of the process team's education and training?
<--- Score

32. Can you adapt and adjust to changing Device Onboarding situations?
<--- Score

33. Is there a documented and implemented monitoring plan?
<--- Score

34. What can you control?
<--- Score

35. Is a response plan in place for when the input, process, or output measures indicate an 'out-of-control' condition?
<--- Score

36. What are the key elements of your Device Onboarding performance improvement system, including your evaluation, organizational learning, and innovation processes?
<--- Score

37. Are the planned controls in place?
<--- Score

38. What other areas of the group might benefit from the Device Onboarding team's improvements, knowledge, and learning?
<--- Score

39. How do senior leaders actions reflect a commitment to the organizations Device Onboarding values?
<--- Score

40. What do your reports reflect?
<--- Score

41. What is the best design framework for Device

Onboarding organization now that, in a post industrial-age if the top-down, command and control model is no longer relevant?
<--- Score

42. Is a response plan established and deployed?
<--- Score

43. Who is going to spread your message?
<--- Score

44. What is the control/monitoring plan?
<--- Score

45. How will new or emerging customer needs/requirements be checked/communicated to orient the process toward meeting the new specifications and continually reducing variation?
<--- Score

46. Are pertinent alerts monitored, analyzed and distributed to appropriate personnel?
<--- Score

47. How do controls support value?
<--- Score

48. What is your plan to assess your security risks?
<--- Score

49. How might the group capture best practices and lessons learned so as to leverage improvements?
<--- Score

50. How do you encourage people to take control and responsibility?

<--- Score

51. What are you attempting to measure/monitor?
<--- Score

52. Have new or revised work instructions resulted?
<--- Score

53. Do you monitor the Device Onboarding decisions made and fine tune them as they evolve?
<--- Score

54. How do you select, collect, align, and integrate Device Onboarding data and information for tracking daily operations and overall organizational performance, including progress relative to strategic objectives and action plans?
<--- Score

55. Is there a recommended audit plan for routine surveillance inspections of Device Onboarding's gains?
<--- Score

56. What do you measure to verify effectiveness gains?
<--- Score

57. Will the team be available to assist members in planning investigations?
<--- Score

58. Do you monitor the effectiveness of your Device Onboarding activities?
<--- Score

59. Will any special training be provided for results interpretation?

<--- Score

60. What is your theory of human motivation, and how does your compensation plan fit with that view?

<--- Score

61. What other systems, operations, processes, and infrastructures (hiring practices, staffing, training, incentives/rewards, metrics/dashboards/scorecards, etc.) need updates, additions, changes, or deletions in order to facilitate knowledge transfer and improvements?

<--- Score

62. How likely is the current Device Onboarding plan to come in on schedule or on budget?

<--- Score

63. Are controls in place and consistently applied?

<--- Score

64. Are there documented procedures?

<--- Score

65. How will the day-to-day responsibilities for monitoring and continual improvement be transferred from the improvement team to the process owner?

<--- Score

66. Is there a Device Onboarding Communication plan covering who needs to get what information when?

<--- Score

67. How do you monitor usage and cost?
<--- Score

68. How will the process owner verify improvement in present and future sigma levels, process capabilities?
<--- Score

69. In the case of a Device Onboarding project, the criteria for the audit derive from implementation objectives, an audit of a Device Onboarding project involves assessing whether the recommendations outlined for implementation have been met, can you track that any Device Onboarding project is implemented as planned, and is it working?
<--- Score

70. What should you measure to verify efficiency gains?
<--- Score

71. Are documented procedures clear and easy to follow for the operators?
<--- Score

72. How will the process owner and team be able to hold the gains?
<--- Score

73. Are you measuring, monitoring and predicting Device Onboarding activities to optimize operations and profitability, and enhancing outcomes?
<--- Score

74. Is there documentation that will support the

successful operation of the improvement?
<--- Score

75. How is Device Onboarding project cost planned, managed, monitored?
<--- Score

76. Are the planned controls working?
<--- Score

77. How will report readings be checked to effectively monitor performance?
<--- Score

78. How do you spread information?
<--- Score

79. How will input, process, and output variables be checked to detect for sub-optimal conditions?
<--- Score

80. Where do ideas that reach policy makers and planners as proposals for Device Onboarding strengthening and reform actually originate?
<--- Score

81. Does Device Onboarding appropriately measure and monitor risk?
<--- Score

82. Implementation Planning: is a pilot needed to test the changes before a full roll out occurs?
<--- Score

83. Is there a control plan in place for sustaining improvements (short and long-term)?

<--- Score

84. Are the Device Onboarding standards challenging?
<--- Score

85. Is there a standardized process?
<--- Score

86. You may have created your quality measures at a time when you lacked resources, technology wasn't up to the required standard, or low service levels were the industry norm. Have those circumstances changed?
<--- Score

87. Who has control over resources?
<--- Score

88. Does a troubleshooting guide exist or is it needed?
<--- Score

89. Against what alternative is success being measured?
<--- Score

90. What should the next improvement project be that is related to Device Onboarding?
<--- Score

91. Who controls critical resources?
<--- Score

92. What key inputs and outputs are being measured on an ongoing basis?
<--- Score

93. How can you best use all of your knowledge repositories to enhance learning and sharing?
<--- Score

94. What are the known security controls?
<--- Score

95. Has the improved process and its steps been standardized?
<--- Score

96. Are suggested corrective/restorative actions indicated on the response plan for known causes to problems that might surface?
<--- Score

97. What do you stand for--and what are you against?
<--- Score

98. How do you establish and deploy modified action plans if circumstances require a shift in plans and rapid execution of new plans?
<--- Score

99. How will Device Onboarding decisions be made and monitored?
<--- Score

Add up total points for this section:
_____ = Total points for this section

Divided by: _____ (number of statements answered) = _____
Average score for this section

Transfer your score to the Device
Onboarding Index at the beginning of
the Self-Assessment.

CRITERION #7: SUSTAIN:

INTENT: Retain the benefits.

In my belief, the answer to this question is clearly defined:

5 Strongly Agree

4 Agree

3 Neutral

2 Disagree

1 Strongly Disagree

1. Who is responsible for ensuring appropriate resources (time, people and money) are allocated to Device Onboarding?
<--- Score

2. Has implementation been effective in reaching specified objectives so far?
<--- Score

3. Who are your customers?
<--- Score

4. Do you have enough freaky customers in your portfolio pushing you to the limit day in and day out?
<--- Score

5. How is implementation research currently incorporated into each of your goals?
<--- Score

6. Who is responsible for errors?
<--- Score

7. If you do not follow, then how to lead?
<--- Score

8. What potential megatrends could make your business model obsolete?
<--- Score

9. If your customer were your grandmother, would you tell her to buy what you're selling?
<--- Score

10. What is the funding source for this project?
<--- Score

11. Why is Device Onboarding important for you now?
<--- Score

12. Do you have an implicit bias for capital investments over people investments?
<--- Score

13. Do you see more potential in people than they do in themselves?

<--- Score

14. Who are four people whose careers you have enhanced?
<--- Score

15. How do you create buy-in?
<--- Score

16. What is the estimated value of the project?
<--- Score

17. How likely is it that a customer would recommend your company to a friend or colleague?
<--- Score

18. Operational - will it work?
<--- Score

19. Marketing budgets are tighter, consumers are more skeptical, and social media has changed forever the way we talk about Device Onboarding, how do you gain traction?
<--- Score

20. What are your most important goals for the strategic Device Onboarding objectives?
<--- Score

21. If no one would ever find out about your accomplishments, how would you lead differently?
<--- Score

22. What would you recommend your friend do if he/she were facing this dilemma?
<--- Score

23. Are you making progress, and are you making progress as Device Onboarding leaders?
<--- Score

24. If your company went out of business tomorrow, would anyone who doesn't get a paycheck here care?
<--- Score

25. At what moment would you think; Will I get fired?
<--- Score

26. What are the long-term Device Onboarding goals?
<--- Score

27. What happens if you do not have enough funding?
<--- Score

28. How are you doing compared to your industry?
<--- Score

29. How do you foster the skills, knowledge, talents, attributes, and characteristics you want to have?
<--- Score

30. What are the key enablers to make this Device Onboarding move?
<--- Score

31. Whom among your colleagues do you trust, and for what?
<--- Score

32. Which individuals, teams or departments will be

involved in Device Onboarding?

<--- Score

33. What could happen if you do not do it?

<--- Score

34. What is your BATNA (best alternative to a negotiated agreement)?

<--- Score

35. Do you think you know, or do you know you know ?

<--- Score

36. What are the essentials of internal Device Onboarding management?

<--- Score

37. Ask yourself: how would you do this work if you only had one staff member to do it?

<--- Score

38. What is the source of the strategies for Device Onboarding strengthening and reform?

<--- Score

39. How can you incorporate support to ensure safe and effective use of Device Onboarding into the services that you provide?

<--- Score

40. If you got fired and a new hire took your place, what would she do different?

<--- Score

41. What new services of functionality will be

implemented next with Device Onboarding ?
<--- Score

42. Are all key stakeholders present at all Structured Walkthroughs?
<--- Score

43. How do you know if you are successful?
<--- Score

44. Do Device Onboarding rules make a reasonable demand on a users capabilities?
<--- Score

45. Whose voice (department, ethnic group, women, older workers, etc) might you have missed hearing from in your company, and how might you amplify this voice to create positive momentum for your business?
<--- Score

46. What is the range of capabilities?
<--- Score

47. Why is it important to have senior management support for a Device Onboarding project?
<--- Score

48. What are the challenges?
<--- Score

49. How do you determine the key elements that affect Device Onboarding workforce satisfaction, how are these elements determined for different workforce groups and segments?

<--- Score

50. What stupid rule would you most like to kill?
<--- Score

51. Are the criteria for selecting recommendations stated?
<--- Score

52. What is the big Device Onboarding idea?
<--- Score

53. How do you deal with Device Onboarding changes?
<--- Score

54. Can you do all this work?
<--- Score

55. How do you keep records, of what?
<--- Score

56. Is there any reason to believe the opposite of my current belief?
<--- Score

57. Who are the key stakeholders?
<--- Score

58. Are you changing as fast as the world around you?
<--- Score

59. What trophy do you want on your mantle?
<--- Score

60. Are the assumptions believable and achievable?

<--- Score

61. How do you foster innovation?
<--- Score

62. Where can you break convention?
<--- Score

63. How can you become the company that would put you out of business?
<--- Score

64. Can the schedule be done in the given time?
<--- Score

65. What are the success criteria that will indicate that Device Onboarding objectives have been met and the benefits delivered?
<--- Score

66. Who do you want your customers to become?
<--- Score

67. What is something you believe that nearly no one agrees with you on?
<--- Score

68. What relationships among Device Onboarding trends do you perceive?
<--- Score

69. What are your personal philosophies regarding Device Onboarding and how do they influence your work?
<--- Score

70. How will you insure seamless interoperability of Device Onboarding moving forward?

<--- Score

71. Is Device Onboarding dependent on the successful delivery of a current project?

<--- Score

72. How much contingency will be available in the budget?

<--- Score

73. What are the potential basics of Device Onboarding fraud?

<--- Score

74. How do you stay inspired?

<--- Score

75. What are specific Device Onboarding rules to follow?

<--- Score

76. Are you maintaining a past–present–future perspective throughout the Device Onboarding discussion?

<--- Score

77. Is your basic point _____ or _____?

<--- Score

78. If you find that you havent accomplished one of the goals for one of the steps of the Device Onboarding strategy, what will you do to fix it?

<--- Score

79. How do you ensure that implementations of Device Onboarding products are done in a way that ensures safety?

<--- Score

80. In retrospect, of the projects that you pulled the plug on, what percent do you wish had been allowed to keep going, and what percent do you wish had ended earlier?

<--- Score

81. What are the performance and scale of the Device Onboarding tools?

<--- Score

82. Do you think Device Onboarding accomplishes the goals you expect it to accomplish?

<--- Score

83. What are the gaps in your knowledge and experience?

<--- Score

84. Are you using a design thinking approach and integrating Innovation, Device Onboarding Experience, and Brand Value?

<--- Score

85. What are the short and long-term Device Onboarding goals?

<--- Score

86. What do we do when new problems arise?

<--- Score

87. What counts that you are not counting?

<--- Score

88. What are the top 3 things at the forefront of your Device Onboarding agendas for the next 3 years?
<--- Score

89. Is a Device Onboarding team work effort in place?
<--- Score

90. Who will manage the integration of tools?
<--- Score

91. Which Device Onboarding goals are the most important?
<--- Score

92. In the past year, what have you done (or could you have done) to increase the accurate perception of your company/brand as ethical and honest?
<--- Score

93. What will be the consequences to the stakeholder (financial, reputation etc) if Device Onboarding does not go ahead or fails to deliver the objectives?
<--- Score

94. What happens when a new employee joins the organization?
<--- Score

95. What is the craziest thing you can do?
<--- Score

96. What should you stop doing?
<--- Score

97. Who will provide the final approval of Device Onboarding deliverables?

<--- Score

98. How will you ensure you get what you expected?

<--- Score

99. Why not do Device Onboarding?

<--- Score

100. Is it economical; do you have the time and money?

<--- Score

101. If you were responsible for initiating and implementing major changes in your organization, what steps might you take to ensure acceptance of those changes?

<--- Score

102. Instead of going to current contacts for new ideas, what if you reconnected with dormant contacts--the people you used to know? If you were going reactivate a dormant tie, who would it be?

<--- Score

103. What is effective Device Onboarding?

<--- Score

104. How do you keep the momentum going?

<--- Score

105. Who will be responsible for deciding whether Device Onboarding goes ahead or not after the initial

investigations?
<--- Score

106. What does your signature ensure?
<--- Score

107. If there were zero limitations, what would you do differently?
<--- Score

108. What role does communication play in the success or failure of a Device Onboarding project?
<--- Score

109. How will you motivate the stakeholders with the least vested interest?
<--- Score

110. In a project to restructure Device Onboarding outcomes, which stakeholders would you involve?
<--- Score

111. What may be the consequences for the performance of an organization if all stakeholders are not consulted regarding Device Onboarding?
<--- Score

112. How do you make it meaningful in connecting Device Onboarding with what users do day-to-day?
<--- Score

113. Will it be accepted by users?
<--- Score

114. What is an unauthorized commitment?
<--- Score

115. Do you have past Device Onboarding successes?
<--- Score

116. How do you set Device Onboarding stretch targets and how do you get people to not only participate in setting these stretch targets but also that they strive to achieve these?
<--- Score

117. What is the overall business strategy?
<--- Score

118. How important is Device Onboarding to the user organizations mission?
<--- Score

119. What is the kind of project structure that would be appropriate for your Device Onboarding project, should it be formal and complex, or can it be less formal and relatively simple?
<--- Score

120. When information truly is ubiquitous, when reach and connectivity are completely global, when computing resources are infinite, and when a whole new set of impossibilities are not only possible, but happening, what will that do to your business?
<--- Score

121. What is it like to work for you?
<--- Score

122. What have you done to protect your business from competitive encroachment?
<--- Score

123. How do you assess the Device Onboarding pitfalls that are inherent in implementing it?

<--- Score

124. Is the Device Onboarding organization completing tasks effectively and efficiently?

<--- Score

125. How do you accomplish your long range Device Onboarding goals?

<--- Score

126. How can you negotiate Device Onboarding successfully with a stubborn boss, an irate client, or a deceitful coworker?

<--- Score

127. Which models, tools and techniques are necessary?

<--- Score

128. What is the recommended frequency of auditing?

<--- Score

129. Are you paying enough attention to the partners your company depends on to succeed?

<--- Score

130. Were lessons learned captured and communicated?

<--- Score

131. How do you maintain Device Onboarding's Integrity?

<--- Score

132. What knowledge, skills and characteristics mark a good Device Onboarding project manager?
<--- Score

133. Can you maintain your growth without detracting from the factors that have contributed to your success?
<--- Score

134. What is the purpose of Device Onboarding in relation to the mission?
<--- Score

135. What is your formula for success in Device Onboarding ?
<--- Score

136. Who do we want your customers to become?
<--- Score

137. Political -is anyone trying to undermine this project?
<--- Score

138. Who is responsible for Device Onboarding?
<--- Score

139. What are the usability implications of Device Onboarding actions?
<--- Score

140. Are you relevant? Will you be relevant five years from now? Ten?
<--- Score

141. What information is critical to your organization that your executives are ignoring?
<--- Score

142. What goals did you miss?
<--- Score

143. What one word do you want to own in the minds of your customers, employees, and partners?
<--- Score

144. What threat is Device Onboarding addressing?
<--- Score

145. What did you miss in the interview for the worst hire you ever made?
<--- Score

146. Why will customers want to buy your organizations products/services?
<--- Score

147. Is maximizing Device Onboarding protection the same as minimizing Device Onboarding loss?
<--- Score

148. How long will it take to change?
<--- Score

149. How do you listen to customers to obtain actionable information?
<--- Score

150. How much does Device Onboarding help?
<--- Score

151. Are new benefits received and understood?
<--- Score

152. If you had to rebuild your organization without any traditional competitive advantages (i.e., no killer technology, promising research, innovative product/service delivery model, etcetera), how would your people have to approach their work and collaborate together in order to create the necessary conditions for success?
<--- Score

153. How do you manage Device Onboarding Knowledge Management (KM)?
<--- Score

154. To whom do you add value?
<--- Score

155. Who uses your product in ways you never expected?
<--- Score

156. Have new benefits been realized?
<--- Score

157. How do you cross-sell and up-sell your Device Onboarding success?
<--- Score

158. What are the barriers to increased Device Onboarding production?
<--- Score

159. Which functions and people interact with the supplier and or customer?
<--- Score

160. Do you know what you are doing? And who do you call if you don't?
<--- Score

161. How can you become more high-tech but still be high touch?
<--- Score

162. Do you have the right capabilities and capacities?
<--- Score

163. What was the last experiment you ran?
<--- Score

164. What business benefits will Device Onboarding goals deliver if achieved?
<--- Score

165. Can you break it down?
<--- Score

166. Is Device Onboarding realistic, or are you setting yourself up for failure?
<--- Score

167. Did your employees make progress today?
<--- Score

168. How do you proactively clarify deliverables and Device Onboarding quality expectations?
<--- Score

169. Do you know who is a friend or a foe?
<--- Score

170. What unique value proposition (UVP) do you offer?
<--- Score

171. Are your responses positive or negative?
<--- Score

172. Would you rather sell to knowledgeable and informed customers or to uninformed customers?
<--- Score

173. Is there a work around that you can use?
<--- Score

174. What would have to be true for the option on the table to be the best possible choice?
<--- Score

175. If you weren't already in this business, would you enter it today? And if not, what are you going to do about it?
<--- Score

176. Are you / should you be revolutionary or evolutionary?
<--- Score

177. Is there any existing Device Onboarding governance structure?
<--- Score

178. What projects are going on in the organization

today, and what resources are those projects using from the resource pools?

<--- Score

179. Are you satisfied with your current role? If not, what is missing from it?

<--- Score

180. How do you transition from the baseline to the target?

<--- Score

181. What are the business goals Device Onboarding is aiming to achieve?

<--- Score

182. Do you have the right people on the bus?

<--- Score

183. Are there any activities that you can take off your to do list?

<--- Score

184. Who is the main stakeholder, with ultimate responsibility for driving Device Onboarding forward?

<--- Score

185. Have benefits been optimized with all key stakeholders?

<--- Score

186. What have been your experiences in defining long range Device Onboarding goals?

<--- Score

187. How do you provide a safe environment -physically and emotionally?
<--- Score

188. Why should people listen to you?
<--- Score

189. Who do you think the world wants your organization to be?
<--- Score

190. Who else should you help?
<--- Score

191. How do you govern and fulfill your societal responsibilities?
<--- Score

192. Do you say no to customers for no reason?
<--- Score

193. What is your Device Onboarding strategy?
<--- Score

194. Is a Device Onboarding breakthrough on the horizon?
<--- Score

195. How will you know that the Device Onboarding project has been successful?
<--- Score

196. What is your competitive advantage?
<--- Score

197. What are the rules and assumptions your industry

operates under? What if the opposite were true?
<--- Score

198. How do you go about securing Device Onboarding?
<--- Score

199. How do senior leaders deploy your organizations vision and values through your leadership system, to the workforce, to key suppliers and partners, and to customers and other stakeholders, as appropriate?
<--- Score

200. What are internal and external Device Onboarding relations?
<--- Score

201. How do you lead with Device Onboarding in mind?
<--- Score

202. Why do and why don't your customers like your organization?
<--- Score

203. What is a feasible sequencing of reform initiatives over time?
<--- Score

204. What are strategies for increasing support and reducing opposition?
<--- Score

205. What is your question? Why?
<--- Score

206. What happens at your organization when people fail?

<--- Score

207. If you had to leave your organization for a year and the only communication you could have with employees/colleagues was a single paragraph, what would you write?

<--- Score

208. Are assumptions made in Device Onboarding stated explicitly?

<--- Score

209. What management system can you use to leverage the Device Onboarding experience, ideas, and concerns of the people closest to the work to be done?

<--- Score

210. What are current Device Onboarding paradigms?

<--- Score

211. What is the overall talent health of your organization as a whole at senior levels, and for each organization reporting to a member of the Senior Leadership Team?

<--- Score

Add up total points for this section:

_ _ _ _ _ = Total points for this section

Divided by: _ _ _ _ _ _ (number of statements answered) = _ _ _ _ _ _ Average score for this section

Transfer your score to the Device
Onboarding Index at the beginning of
the Self-Assessment.

Device Onboarding and Managing Projects, Criteria for Project Managers:

1.0 Initiating Process Group: Device Onboarding

1. Were resources available as planned?

2. What are the pressing issues of the hour?

3. Are identified risks being monitored properly, are new risks arising during the Device Onboarding project or are foreseen risks occurring?

4. Who is behind the Device Onboarding project?

5. Were decisions made in a timely manner?

6. Contingency planning. if a risk event occurs, what will you do?

7. How well did the chosen processes produce the expected results?

8. Are the changes in your Device Onboarding project being formally requested, analyzed, and approved by the appropriate decision makers?

9. Does the Device Onboarding project team have enough people to execute the Device Onboarding project plan?

10. Which six sigma dmaic phase focuses on why and how defects and errors occur?

11. Who does what?

12. Which of six sigmas dmaic phases focuses on the

measurement of internal process that affect factors that are critical to quality?

13. Do you know all the stakeholders impacted by the Device Onboarding project and what needs are?

14. Are you properly tracking the progress of the Device Onboarding project and communicating the status to stakeholders?

15. When must it be done?

16. At which cmmi level are software processes documented, standardized, and integrated into a standard to-be practiced process for your organization?

17. What are the constraints?

18. Who are the Device Onboarding project stakeholders?

19. Have the stakeholders identified all individual requirements pertaining to business process?

20. At which stage, in a typical Device Onboarding project do stake holders have maximum influence?

1.1 Project Charter: Device Onboarding

21. How high should you set your goals?

22. What is in it for you?

23. What are the deliverables?

24. What are the assigned resources?

25. Customer benefits: what customer requirements does this Device Onboarding project address?

26. Who are the stakeholders?

27. When do you use a Device Onboarding project Charter?

28. Who manages integration?

29. What metrics could you look at?

30. Who will take notes, document decisions?

31. When is a charter needed?

32. What is the purpose of the Device Onboarding project?

33. What does it need to do?

34. Fit with other Products Compliments –

Cannibalizes?

35. Where does all this information come from?

36. What is the justification?

37. Why use a Device Onboarding project charter?

38. If finished, on what date did it finish?

39. Strategic fit: what is the strategic initiative identifier for this Device Onboarding project?

40. Why the improvements?

1.2 Stakeholder Register: Device Onboarding

41. What is the power of the stakeholder?

42. Who wants to talk about Security?

43. How much influence do they have on the Device Onboarding project?

44. What opportunities exist to provide communications?

45. Who is managing stakeholder engagement?

46. Is your organization ready for change?

47. How should employers make voices heard?

48. What & Why?

49. How big is the gap?

50. How will reports be created?

51. What are the major Device Onboarding project milestones requiring communications or providing communications opportunities?

1.3 Stakeholder Analysis Matrix: Device Onboarding

52. Effects on core activities, distraction?

53. What do you need to appraise?

54. What unique or lowest-cost resources does the Device Onboarding project have access to?

55. What are the reimbursement requirements?

56. Disadvantages of proposition?

57. Alliances: with which other actors is the actor allied, how are they interconnected?

58. What is the stakeholders name, what is function?

59. What tools would help you communicate?

60. Advantages of proposition?

61. What is the range you need to look at?

62. Legislative effects?

63. What is your Advocacy Strategy?

64. Is there evidence that demonstrates the impact of education on the Device Onboarding projects outcomes?

65. Cultural, attitudinal, behavioural?

66. How do customers express needs?

67. Are there people who ise voices or interests in the issue may not be heard?

68. What are the mechanisms of public and social accountability, and how can they be made better?

69. Does your organization have bad debt or cash-flow problems?

70. What actions can be taken to reduce or mitigate risk?

71. Marketing - reach, distribution, awareness?

2.0 Planning Process Group: Device Onboarding

72. To what extent are the visions and actions of the partners consistent or divergent with regard to the program?

73. To what extent and in what ways are the Device Onboarding project contributing to progress towards organizational reform?

74. If action is called for, what form should it take?

75. How are the principles of aid effectiveness (ownership, alignment, management for development results and mutual responsibility) being applied in the Device Onboarding project?

76. What good practices or successful experiences or transferable examples have been identified?

77. Did you read it correctly?

78. What is the difference between the early schedule and late schedule?

79. To what extent is the program helping to influence your organizations policy framework?

80. To what extent has a PMO contributed to raising the quality of the design of the Device Onboarding project?

81. How should needs be met?

82. To what extent have the target population and participants made the activities own, taking an active role in it?

83. What makes your Device Onboarding project successful?

84. What type of estimation method are you using?

85. What will you do?

86. How does activity resource estimation affect activity duration estimation?

87. To what extent are the participating departments coordinating with each other?

88. Device Onboarding project assessment; why did you do this Device Onboarding project?

89. Have more efficient (sensitive) and appropriate measures been adopted to respond to the political and socio-cultural problems identified?

90. What should you do next?

2.1 Project Management Plan: Device Onboarding

91. Will you add a schedule and diagram?

92. What happened during the process that you found interesting?

93. What is Device Onboarding project scope management?

94. What goes into your Device Onboarding project Charter?

95. How do you manage integration?

96. When is the Device Onboarding project management plan created?

97. How well are you able to manage your risk?

98. What are the known stakeholder requirements?

99. What worked well?

100. What went wrong?

101. Why Change?

102. Are there any windfall benefits that would accrue to the Device Onboarding project sponsor or other parties?

103. What data/reports/tools/etc. do program managers need?

104. What if, for example, the positive direction and vision of your organization causes expected trends to change resulting in greater need than expected?

105. What are the training needs?

106. Is mitigation authorized or recommended?

107. Are there any client staffing expectations?

2.2 Scope Management Plan: Device Onboarding

108. What are the risks that could significantly affect the communication on the Device Onboarding project?

109. Has your organization done similar tasks before?

110. Pareto diagrams, statistical sampling, flow charting or trend analysis used quality monitoring?

111. Has the budget been baselined?

112. Will anyone else be involved in verifying the deliverables?

113. Are you meeting with stake holders and team members?

114. Are all key components of a Quality Assurance Plan present?

115. Have all unresolved risks been documented?

116. Does the quality assurance process provide objective verification of adherence to applicable standards, procedures & requirements?

117. How do you plan to control Scope Creep?

118. Is stakeholder involvement adequate?

119. Are risk triggers captured?

120. What if you do not have more detailed information on the report?

121. When will scope verification be performed?

122. Are vendor contract reports, reviews and visits conducted periodically?

123. Are issues raised, assessed, actioned, and resolved in a timely and efficient manner?

124. Describe the process for rejecting the Device Onboarding project deliverables. What happens to rejected deliverables?

125. Does the detailed work plan match the complexity of tasks with the capabilities of personnel?

126. Has the Device Onboarding project approach and development strategy of the Device Onboarding project been defined, documented and accepted by the appropriate stakeholders?

127. Do you secure formal approval of changes and requirements from stakeholders?

2.3 Requirements Management Plan: Device Onboarding

128. Is the system software (non-operating system) new to the IT Device Onboarding project team?

129. How will you develop the schedule of requirements activities?

130. Who has the authority to reject Device Onboarding project requirements?

131. If it exists, where is it housed?

132. Will you document changes to requirements?

133. Did you use declarative statements?

134. How often will the reporting occur?

135. The wbs is developed as part of a joint planning session. and how do you know that youhave done this right?

136. What is the earliest finish date for this Device Onboarding project if it is scheduled to start on ...?

137. Did you avoid subjective, flowery or non-specific statements?

138. What went right?

139. Who will initially review the Device Onboarding

project work or products to ensure it meets the applicable acceptance criteria?

140. Will you have access to stakeholders when you need them?

141. Who will do the reporting and to whom will reports be delivered?

142. Is requirements work dependent on any other specific Device Onboarding project or non-Device Onboarding project activities (e.g. funding, approvals, procurement)?

143. Who will perform the analysis?

144. What are you trying to do?

145. Did you provide clear and concise specifications?

146. Will you perform a Requirements Risk assessment and develop a plan to deal with risks?

147. Do you expect stakeholders to be cooperative?

2.4 Requirements Documentation: Device Onboarding

148. What will be the integration problems?

149. Who is interacting with the system?

150. Can the requirement be changed without a large impact on other requirements?

151. How much testing do you need to do to prove that your system is safe?

152. Does your organization restrict technical alternatives?

153. What are the potential disadvantages/ advantages?

154. Where do you define what is a customer, what are the attributes of customer?

155. How will requirements be documented and who signs off on them?

156. What can tools do for us?

157. What are current process problems?

158. What is the risk associated with the technology?

159. Consistency. are there any requirements conflicts?

160. Basic work/business process; high-level, what is being touched?

161. What are the acceptance criteria?

162. Where do system and software requirements come from, what are sources?

163. If applicable; are there issues linked with the fact that this is an offshore Device Onboarding project?

164. Can the requirements be checked?

165. What is a show stopper in the requirements?

166. How does what is being described meet the business need?

167. Is the origin of the requirement clearly stated?

2.5 Requirements Traceability Matrix: Device Onboarding

168. Is there a requirements traceability process in place?

169. What is the WBS?

170. What percentage of Device Onboarding projects are producing traceability matrices between requirements and other work products?

171. Describe the process for approving requirements so they can be added to the traceability matrix and Device Onboarding project work can be performed. Will the Device Onboarding project requirements become approved in writing?

172. How will it affect the stakeholders personally in career?

173. Why use a WBS?

174. Do you have a clear understanding of all subcontracts in place?

175. How do you manage scope?

176. How small is small enough?

177. Why do you manage scope?

178. Will you use a Requirements Traceability Matrix?

179. What are the chronologies, contingencies, consequences, criteria?

2.6 Project Scope Statement: Device Onboarding

180. Relevant - ask yourself can you get there; why are you doing this Device Onboarding project?

181. Is an issue management process documented and filed?

182. Is the scope of your Device Onboarding project well defined?

183. What process would you recommend for creating the Device Onboarding project scope statement?

184. What is the most common tool for helping define the detail?

185. Change management vs. change leadership - what is the difference?

186. Is the plan for your organization of the Device Onboarding project resources adequate?

187. What are the possible consequences should a risk come to occur?

188. What are the defined meeting materials?

189. Have you been able to thoroughly document the Device Onboarding projects assumptions and constraints?

190. Was planning completed before the Device Onboarding project was initiated?

191. Are there completion/verification criteria defined for each task producing an output?

192. Will the risk documents be filed?

193. Is the change control process documented and on file?

194. Have the configuration management functions been assigned?

195. What is change?

196. Are there backup strategies for key members of the Device Onboarding project?

2.7 Assumption and Constraint Log: Device Onboarding

197. If appropriate, is the deliverable content consistent with current Device Onboarding project documents and in compliance with the Document Management Plan?

198. Does the traceability documentation describe the tool and/or mechanism to be used to capture traceability throughout the life cycle?

199. How are new requirements or changes to requirements identified?

200. What does an audit system look like?

201. Can the requirements be traced to the appropriate components of the solution, as well as test scripts?

202. Has the approach and development strategy of the Device Onboarding project been defined, documented and accepted by the appropriate stakeholders?

203. What strengths do you have?

204. What other teams / processes would be impacted by changes to the current process, and how?

205. Security analysis has access to information that is sanitized?

206. Diagrams and tables are included to account for complex concepts and increase overall readability?

207. How relevant is this attribute to this Device Onboarding project or audit?

208. Are formal code reviews conducted?

209. How many Device Onboarding project staff does this specific process affect?

210. Are there standards for code development?

211. What threats might prevent you from getting there?

212. Have adequate resources been provided by management to ensure Device Onboarding project success?

213. How can you prevent/fix violations?

214. What weaknesses do you have?

215. Is the current scope of the Device Onboarding project substantially different than that originally defined in the approved Device Onboarding project plan?

2.8 Work Breakdown Structure: Device Onboarding

216. When do you stop?

217. When does it have to be done?

218. What has to be done?

219. Do you need another level?

220. How big is a work-package?

221. Why would you develop a Work Breakdown Structure?

222. Is the work breakdown structure (wbs) defined and is the scope of the Device Onboarding project clear with assigned deliverable owners?

223. How will you and your Device Onboarding project team define the Device Onboarding projects scope and work breakdown structure?

224. Is it a change in scope?

225. How many levels?

226. Who has to do it?

227. Why is it useful?

228. Is it still viable?

229. Where does it take place?

230. Can you make it?

231. How much detail?

232. What is the probability that the Device Onboarding project duration will exceed xx weeks?

2.9 WBS Dictionary: Device Onboarding

233. Does the contractors system provide for determination of price variance by comparing planned Vs actual commitments?

234. Authorization to proceed with all authorized work?

235. Are internal budgets for authorized, and not priced changes based on the contractors resource plan for accomplishing the work?

236. Are estimates of costs at completion generated in a rational, consistent manner?

237. Does the contractors system description or procedures require that the performance measurement baseline plus management reserve equal the contract budget base?

238. Are the rates for allocating costs from each indirect cost pool to contracts updated as necessary to ensure a realistic monthly allocation of indirect costs without significant year-end adjustments?

239. Are budgets or values assigned to work packages and planning packages in terms of dollars, hours, or other measurable units?

240. Are data elements (BCWS, BCWP, and ACWP) progressively summarized from the detail level to the

contract level through the CWBS?

241. Are Device Onboarding projected overhead costs in each pool and the associated direct costs used as the basis for establishing interim rates for allocating overhead to contracts?

242. Should you include sub-activities?

243. Is cost performance measurement at the point in time most suitable for the category of material involved, and no earlier than the time of actual receipt of material?

244. Software specification, development, integration, and testing, licenses ?

245. The already stated responsible for overhead performance control of related costs?

246. What is wrong with this Device Onboarding project?

247. Are data being used by managers in an effective manner to ascertain Device Onboarding project or functional status, to identify reasons or significant variance, and to initiate appropriate corrective action?

248. Is the entire contract planned in time-phased control accounts to the extent practicable?

249. Does the contractors system provide for the determination of cost variances attributable to the excess usage of material?

250. What is the end result of a work package?

251. Should you have a test for each code module?

2.10 Schedule Management Plan: Device Onboarding

252. Is the schedule updated on a periodic basis?

253. Is there a formal set of procedures supporting Issues Management?

254. Is current scope of the Device Onboarding project substantially different than that originally defined?

255. Cost / benefit analysis?

256. Has a quality assurance plan been developed for the Device Onboarding project?

257. Will the Device Onboarding project sponsor be involved in preliminary schedule reviews?

258. Is there a set of procedures defining the scope, procedures, and deliverables defining quality control?

259. Have stakeholder accountabilities & responsibilities been clearly defined?

260. After initial schedule development, will the schedule be reviewed and validated by the Device Onboarding project team?

261. Is there general agreement & acceptance of the current status and progress of the Device Onboarding project?

262. Have adequate resources been provided by management to ensure Device Onboarding project success?

263. Has a provision been made to reassess Device Onboarding project risks at various Device Onboarding project stages?

264. Does the Device Onboarding project have a Quality Culture?

265. Have activity relationships and interdependencies within tasks been adequately identified?

266. Is there an on-going process in place to monitor Device Onboarding project risks?

267. Has the business need been clearly defined?

268. Is the critical path valid?

269. Is a process for scheduling and reporting defined, including forms and formats?

270. Does the schedule have reasonable float?

2.11 Activity List: Device Onboarding

271. How should ongoing costs be monitored to try to keep the Device Onboarding project within budget?

272. What went well?

273. What is your organizations history in doing similar activities?

274. How do you determine the late start (LS) for each activity?

275. What is the probability the Device Onboarding project can be completed in xx weeks?

276. How can the Device Onboarding project be displayed graphically to better visualize the activities?

277. Is there anything planned that does not need to be here?

278. Can you determine the activity that must finish, before this activity can start?

279. What is the LF and LS for each activity?

280. What did not go as well?

281. In what sequence?

282. How will it be performed?

283. What are you counting on?

284. Who will perform the work?

285. Are the required resources available or need to be acquired?

286. How much slack is available in the Device Onboarding project?

287. How detailed should a Device Onboarding project get?

2.12 Activity Attributes: Device Onboarding

288. Activity: what is Missing?

289. Has management defined a definite timeframe for the turnaround or Device Onboarding project window?

290. What is missing?

291. What activity do you think you should spend the most time on?

292. Do you feel very comfortable with your prediction?

293. How many resources do you need to complete the work scope within a limit of X number of days?

294. Can more resources be added?

295. How do you manage time?

296. Is there a trend during the year?

297. Have constraints been applied to the start and finish milestones for the phases?

298. Are the required resources available?

299. What is the general pattern here?

300. Resource is assigned to?

301. How difficult will it be to complete specific activities on this Device Onboarding project?

302. Activity: what is In the Bag?

303. Were there other ways you could have organized the data to achieve similar results?

304. What conclusions/generalizations can you draw from this?

305. Where else does it apply?

2.13 Milestone List: Device Onboarding

306. What would happen if a delivery of material was one week late?

307. Identify critical paths (one or more) and which activities are on the critical path?

308. Describe the concept of the technology, product or service that will be or has been developed. How will it be used?

309. Do you foresee any technical risks or developmental challenges?

310. Obstacles faced?

311. When will the Device Onboarding project be complete?

312. Milestone pages should display the UserID of the person who added the milestone. Does a report or query exist that provides this audit information?

313. Continuity, supply chain robustness?

314. Vital contracts and partners?

315. How late can the activity finish?

316. What background experience, skills, and strengths does the team bring to your organization?

317. Describe the industry you are in and the market growth opportunities. What is the market for your technology, product or service?

318. Timescales, deadlines and pressures?

319. How will the milestone be verified?

320. Competitive advantages?

321. Insurmountable weaknesses?

322. Reliability of data, plan predictability?

2.14 Network Diagram: Device Onboarding

323. If the Device Onboarding project network diagram cannot change and you have extra personnel resources, what is the BEST thing to do?

324. How confident can you be in your milestone dates and the delivery date?

325. Which type of network diagram allows you to depict four types of dependencies?

326. If x is long, what would be the completion time if you break x into two parallel parts of y weeks and z weeks?

327. If a current contract exists, can you provide the vendor name, contract start, and contract expiration date?

328. Exercise: what is the probability that the Device Onboarding project duration will exceed xx weeks?

329. Why must you schedule milestones, such as reviews, throughout the Device Onboarding project?

330. What are the Key Success Factors?

331. Will crashing x weeks return more in benefits than it costs?

332. Are you on time?

333. Can you calculate the confidence level?

334. What job or jobs could run concurrently?

335. What to do and When?

336. Are the gantt chart and/or network diagram updated periodically and used to assess the overall Device Onboarding project timetable?

337. How difficult will it be to do specific activities on this Device Onboarding project?

338. Planning: who, how long, what to do?

339. What is the probability of completing the Device Onboarding project in less that xx days?

340. What controls the start and finish of a job?

341. What activities must follow this activity?

2.15 Activity Resource Requirements: Device Onboarding

342. What is the Work Plan Standard?

343. What are constraints that you might find during the Human Resource Planning process?

344. Why do you do that?

345. Time for overtime?

346. Do you use tools like decomposition and rolling-wave planning to produce the activity list and other outputs?

347. Other support in specific areas?

348. How many signatures do you require on a check and does this match what is in your policy and procedures?

349. Organizational Applicability?

350. Anything else?

351. How do you handle petty cash?

352. Which logical relationship does the PDM use most often?

353. When does monitoring begin?

354. Are there unresolved issues that need to be addressed?

2.16 Resource Breakdown Structure: Device Onboarding

355. What is the difference between % Complete and % work?

356. Who will be used as a Device Onboarding project team member?

357. What is the number one predictor of a groups productivity?

358. Why do you do it?

359. What are the requirements for resource data?

360. Who will use the system?

361. Any changes from stakeholders?

362. Who is allowed to perform which functions?

363. Changes based on input from stakeholders?

364. Which resource planning tool provides information on resource responsibility and accountability?

365. How should the information be delivered?

366. Which resources should be in the resource pool?

367. Is predictive resource analysis being done?

368. Why time management?

369. How can this help you with team building?

370. What defines a successful Device Onboarding project?

2.17 Activity Duration Estimates: Device Onboarding

371. Are processes defined to monitor Device Onboarding project cost and schedule variances?

372. What is the critical path for this Device Onboarding project and how long is it?

373. What are the main types of contracts if you do decide to outsource?

374. Why is outsourcing growing so rapidly?

375. Will additional funds be needed for hardware or software?

376. Are Device Onboarding project records organized, maintained, and assessable by Device Onboarding project team members?

377. How difficult will it be to do specific activities on this Device Onboarding project?

378. Why do you think schedule issues often cause the most conflicts on Device Onboarding projects?

379. Are procedures defined for calculating cost estimates?

380. Account for the four frames of organizations. How can they help Device Onboarding project managers understand your organizational context for

Device Onboarding projects?

381. Are Device Onboarding project results verified and Device Onboarding project documents archived?

382. Is earned value analysis completed to assess Device Onboarding project performance?

383. Why is it important to determine activity sequencing on Device Onboarding projects?

384. Is a Device Onboarding project charter created once a Device Onboarding project is formally recognized?

385. What is the shortest possible time it will take to complete this Device Onboarding project?

386. Does the software appear easy to learn?

387. Do they make sense?

388. Which would be the NEXT thing for the Device Onboarding project manager to do?

389. Which is the BEST thing to do to try to complete a Device Onboarding project two days earlier?

390. Does a process exist to determine the probability of risk events?

2.18 Duration Estimating Worksheet: Device Onboarding

391. When do the individual activities need to start and finish?

392. Why estimate time and cost?

393. Is this operation cost effective?

394. How can the Device Onboarding project be displayed graphically to better visualize the activities?

395. For other activities, how much delay can be tolerated?

396. What is your role?

397. What questions do you have?

398. Define the work as completely as possible. What work will be included in the Device Onboarding project?

399. When does your organization expect to be able to complete it?

400. Is the Device Onboarding project responsive to community need?

401. What is the total time required to complete the Device Onboarding project if no delays occur?

402. Small or large Device Onboarding project?

403. Science = process: remember the scientific method?

404. What is next?

405. Value pocket identification & quantification what are value pockets?

406. What are the critical bottleneck activities?

407. Can the Device Onboarding project be constructed as planned?

408. Is a construction detail attached (to aid in explanation)?

2.19 Project Schedule: Device Onboarding

409. Is the Device Onboarding project schedule available for all Device Onboarding project team members to review?

410. Are you working on the right risks?

411. How can you minimize or control changes to Device Onboarding project schedules?

412. Are the original Device Onboarding project schedule and budget realistic?

413. Are all remaining durations correct?

414. What is risk?

415. Understand the constraints used in preparing the schedule. Are activities connected because logic dictates the order in which others occur?

416. How can you address that situation?

417. Why is software Device Onboarding project disaster so common?

418. What is the purpose of a Device Onboarding project schedule?

419. Why or why not?

420. Are there activities that came from a template or previous Device Onboarding project that are not applicable on this phase of this Device Onboarding project?

421. Have all Device Onboarding project delays been adequately accounted for, communicated to all stakeholders and adjustments made in overall Device Onboarding project schedule?

422. If there are any qualifying green components to this Device Onboarding project, what portion of the total Device Onboarding project cost is green?

423. Are activities connected because logic dictates the order in which others occur?

424. How closely did the initial Device Onboarding project Schedule compare with the actual schedule?

2.20 Cost Management Plan: Device Onboarding

425. Are Device Onboarding project contact logs kept up to date?

426. Are estimating assumptions and constraints captured?

427. Does the Device Onboarding project have a Quality Culture?

428. Outside experts?

429. Are the Device Onboarding project team members located locally to the users/stakeholders?

430. What is the work breakdown structure for the Device Onboarding project?

431. Escalation criteria met?

432. Is it possible to track all classes of Device Onboarding project work (e.g. scheduled, un-scheduled, defect repair, etc.)?

433. Eac -estimate at completion, what is the total job expected to cost?

434. What is your organizations history in doing similar tasks?

435. What are the nine areas of expertise?

436. Are procurement deliverables arriving on time and to specification?

437. Are all resource assumptions documented?

438. Have all involved Device Onboarding project stakeholders and work groups committed to the Device Onboarding project?

439. Is pert / critical path or equivalent methodology being used?

440. Was the scope definition used in task sequencing?

2.21 Activity Cost Estimates: Device Onboarding

441. What makes a good expected result statement?

442. Maintenance Reserve?

443. What is Device Onboarding project cost management?

444. Were sponsors and decision makers available when needed outside regularly scheduled meetings?

445. How many activities should you have?

446. What procedures are put in place regarding bidding and cost comparisons, if any?

447. Performance bond should always provide what part of the contract value?

448. Why do you manage cost?

449. If you are asked to lower your estimate because the price is too high, what are your options?

450. Were you satisfied with the work?

451. Vac -variance at completion, how much over/ under budget do you expect to be?

452. Estimated cost?

453. Measurable - are the targets measurable?

454. Were the tasks or work products prepared by the consultant useful?

455. What is the activity inventory?

456. Who determines the quality and expertise of contractors?

457. Scope statement only direct or indirect costs as well?

458. Did the consultant work with local staff to develop local capacity?

459. How do you allocate indirect costs to activities?

2.22 Cost Estimating Worksheet: Device Onboarding

460. What info is needed?

461. What can be included?

462. What will others want?

463. Can a trend be established from historical performance data on the selected measure and are the criteria for using trend analysis or forecasting methods met?

464. How will the results be shared and to whom?

465. Does the Device Onboarding project provide innovative ways for stakeholders to overcome obstacles or deliver better outcomes?

466. Who is best positioned to know and assist in identifying corresponding factors?

467. What costs are to be estimated?

468. What is the estimated labor cost today based upon this information?

469. Identify the timeframe necessary to monitor progress and collect data to determine how the selected measure has changed?

470. Will the Device Onboarding project collaborate

with the local community and leverage resources?

471. What is the purpose of estimating?

472. Is it feasible to establish a control group arrangement?

473. Is the Device Onboarding project responsive to community need?

474. Ask: are others positioned to know, are others credible, and will others cooperate?

475. What additional Device Onboarding project(s) could be initiated as a result of this Device Onboarding project?

476. What happens to any remaining funds not used?

2.23 Cost Baseline: Device Onboarding

477. What can go wrong?

478. Have all approved changes to the Device Onboarding project requirement been identified and impact on the performance, cost, and schedule baselines documented?

479. Who will use corresponding metrics ?

480. How likely is it to go wrong?

481. Is there anything you need from upper management in order to be successful?

482. If you sold 10x widgets on a day, what would the affect on profits be?

483. How fast?

484. Are there contingencies or conditions related to the acceptance?

485. Have all approved changes to the schedule baseline been identified and impact on the Device Onboarding project documented?

486. Has operations management formally accepted responsibility for operating and maintaining the product(s) or service(s) delivered by the Device Onboarding project?

487. Has the documentation relating to operation and maintenance of the product(s) or service(s) been delivered to, and accepted by, operations management?

488. What is it ?

489. What is cost and Device Onboarding project cost management?

490. Will the Device Onboarding project fail if the change request is not executed?

491. How difficult will it be to do specific tasks on the Device Onboarding project?

2.24 Quality Management Plan: Device Onboarding

492. Do trained quality assurance auditors conduct the audits as defined in the Quality Management Plan and scheduled by the Device Onboarding project manager?

493. How are changes to procedures made?

494. Are there nonconformance issues?

495. How do you decide what information needs to be recorded?

496. How many Device Onboarding project staff does this specific process affect?

497. Is there a Quality Management Plan?

498. What process do you use to minimize errors, defects, and rework?

499. What data do you gather/use/compile?

500. Are best practices and metrics employed to identify issues, progress, performance, etc.?

501. What changes can you make that will result in improvement?

502. Is this process still needed?

503. What are your organizations current levels and trends for the already stated measures related to financial and marketplace performance?

504. What is the return on investment?

505. Does the program use modeling in the permitting or decision-making processes?

506. How is staff trained on the recording of field notes?

507. How does your organization design processes to ensure others meet customer and others requirements?

508. Sampling part of task?

509. Contradictory information between document sections?

510. Where do you focus?

511. Are qmps good forever?

2.25 Quality Metrics: Device Onboarding

512. What is the CMS Benchmark?

513. What is the timeline to meet your goal?

514. There are many reasons to shore up quality-related metrics, and what metrics are important?

515. Were quality attributes reported?

516. Are documents on hand to provide explanations of privacy and confidentiality?

517. What documentation is required?

518. Is the reporting frequency appropriate?

519. Is there alignment within your organization on definitions?

520. What does this tell us?

521. Do you stratify metrics by product or site?

522. What makes a visualization memorable?

523. Product Availability ?

524. Did the team meet the Device Onboarding project success criteria documented in the Quality Metrics Matrix?

525. Do the operators focus on determining; is there anything you need to worry about?

526. Which data do others need in one place to target areas of improvement?

527. Why is now the time for quality metrics?

528. What metrics do you measure?

529. Are quality metrics defined?

2.26 Process Improvement Plan: Device Onboarding

530. Have the supporting tools been developed or acquired?

531. Where do you want to be?

532. Management commitment at all levels?

533. Have the frequency of collection and the points in the process where measurements will be made been determined?

534. What personnel are the coaches for your initiative?

535. What lessons have you learned so far?

536. Everyone agrees on what process improvement is, right?

537. What personnel are the champions for the initiative?

538. Are you making progress on your improvement plan?

539. How do you measure?

540. Why do you want to achieve the goal?

541. Are you making progress on the goals?

542. The motive is determined by asking, Why do you want to achieve this goal?

543. Purpose of goal: the motive is determined by asking, why do you want to achieve this goal?

544. What actions are needed to address the problems and achieve the goals?

545. Have storage and access mechanisms and procedures been determined?

546. What makes people good SPI coaches?

547. What personnel are the sponsors for that initiative?

2.27 Responsibility Assignment Matrix: Device Onboarding

548. Are others working on the right things?

549. Is accountability placed at the lowest-possible level within the Device Onboarding project so that decisions can be made at that level?

550. Too many as: does a proper segregation of duties exist?

551. Does the contractors system provide unit or lot costs when applicable?

552. What do you need to implement earned value management?

553. Does the contractor use objective results, design reviews and tests to trace schedule performance?

554. What travel needed?

555. What simple tool can you use to help identify and prioritize Device Onboarding project risks that is very low tech and high touch?

556. When performing is split among two or more roles, is the work clearly defined so that the efforts are coordinated and the communication is clear?

557. Is work progressively subdivided into detailed work packages as requirements are defined?

558. Are meaningful indicators identified for use in measuring the status of cost and schedule performance?

559. Availability – will the group or the person be available within the necessary time interval?

560. All cwbs elements specified for external reporting?

561. Does the accounting system provide a basis for auditing records of direct costs chargeable to the contract?

562. Are data elements reconcilable between internal summary reports and reports forwarded to stakeholders?

563. Are people encouraged to bring up issues?

564. Are overhead costs budgets established on a basis consistent with anticipated direct business base?

2.28 Roles and Responsibilities: Device Onboarding

565. Is the data complete?

566. Have you ever been a part of this team?

567. Implementation of actions: Who are the responsible units?

568. Is feedback clearly communicated and non-judgmental?

569. Who is responsible for each task?

570. What areas would you highlight for changes or improvements?

571. Where are you most strong as a supervisor?

572. What is working well?

573. Are your policies supportive of a culture of quality data?

574. Once the responsibilities are defined for the Device Onboarding project, have the deliverables, roles and responsibilities been clearly communicated to every participant?

575. What should you do now to ensure that you are meeting all expectations of your current position?

576. Does the team have access to and ability to use data analysis tools?

577. What specific behaviors did you observe?

578. To decide whether to use a quality measurement, ask how will you know when it is achieved?

579. Concern: where are you limited or have no authority, where you can not influence?

580. What should you do now to ensure that you are exceeding expectations and excelling in your current position?

581. Who is involved?

582. Are Device Onboarding project team roles and responsibilities identified and documented?

583. Was the expectation clearly communicated?

584. Key conclusions and recommendations: Are conclusions and recommendations relevant and acceptable?

2.29 Human Resource Management Plan: Device Onboarding

585. Is there a formal set of procedures supporting Stakeholder Management?

586. How to convince to employees that it is a necessary process?

587. Is the manpower level sufficient to meet the future business requirements?

588. What commitments have been made?

589. Is the Device Onboarding project schedule available for all Device Onboarding project team members to review?

590. How can below standard performers be guided/developed to upgrade performance?

591. Have the key functions and capabilities been defined and assigned to each release or iteration?

592. How does the proposed individual meet each requirement?

593. Are the payment terms being followed?

594. Have process improvement efforts been completed before requirements efforts begin?

595. Has the schedule been baselined?

596. Is your organization human?

597. Are all payments made according to the contract(s)?

598. Is Device Onboarding project work proceeding in accordance with the original Device Onboarding project schedule?

599. Are governance roles and responsibilities documented?

600. Are meeting objectives identified for each meeting?

601. How well does your organization communicate?

2.30 Communications Management Plan: Device Onboarding

602. Who have you worked with in past, similar initiatives?

603. Who is involved as you identify stakeholders?

604. Who needs to know and how much?

605. Who will use or be affected by the result of a Device Onboarding project?

606. What does the stakeholder need from the team?

607. What is the stakeholders level of authority?

608. What approaches do you use?

609. Are stakeholders internal or external?

610. Will messages be directly related to the release strategy or phases of the Device Onboarding project?

611. Can you think of other people who might have concerns or interests?

612. What to learn?

613. Are others part of the communications management plan?

614. Are there potential barriers between the team

and the stakeholder?

615. Which stakeholders can influence others?

616. Why is stakeholder engagement important?

617. How much time does it take to do it?

618. Do you then often overlook a key stakeholder or stakeholder group?

619. How did the term stakeholder originate?

620. Are there too many who have an interest in some aspect of your work?

2.31 Risk Management Plan: Device Onboarding

621. What is the impact to the Device Onboarding project if the item is not resolved in a timely fashion?

622. Premium on reliability of product?

623. Could others have been better mitigated?

624. Why do you want risk management?

625. Risk documentation: what reporting formats and processes will be used for risk management activities?

626. Are the metrics meaningful and useful?

627. Is the customer willing to commit significant time to the requirements gathering process?

628. Is this an issue, action item, question or a risk?

629. What can you do to minimize the impact if it does?

630. Why is product liability a serious issue?

631. Risk categories: what are the main categories of risks that should be addressed on this Device Onboarding project?

632. What would you do differently?

633. Minimize cost and financial risk?

634. Do you train all developers in the process?

635. Where do risks appear in the business phases?

636. What things might go wrong?

637. Are you on schedule?

638. Is the technology to be built new to your organization?

639. Havent software Device Onboarding projects been late before?

640. Market risk: will the new product be useful to your organization or marketable to others?

2.32 Risk Register: Device Onboarding

641. What is a Risk?

642. Do you require further engagement?

643. Risk probability and impact: how will the probabilities and impacts of risk items be assessed?

644. Severity Prediction?

645. What may happen or not go according to plan?

646. Are there any knock-on effects/impact on any of the other areas?

647. What are your key risks/show istoppers and what is being done to manage them?

648. What action, if any, has been taken to respond to the risk?

649. Are there any gaps in the evidence?

650. What is a Community Risk Register?

651. Who is going to do it?

652. What should you do now?

653. Are there other alternative controls that could be implemented?

654. People risk -are people with appropriate skills

available to help complete the Device Onboarding project?

655. What will be done?

656. What should the audit role be in establishing a risk management process?

657. Does the evidence highlight any areas to advance opportunities or foster good relations. If yes what steps will be taken?

658. What has changed since the last period?

659. How is a Community Risk Register created?

2.33 Probability and Impact Assessment: Device Onboarding

660. Why has this particular mode of contracting been chosen?

661. Who will be in command to monitor and control the performance of the consortium members (consortium leader/client)?

662. Assuming that you have identified a number of risks in the Device Onboarding project, how would you prioritize them?

663. What should be the gestation period for the Device Onboarding project with specific technology?

664. How completely has the customer been identified?

665. What are the chances the event will occur?

666. Do you have a consistent repeatable process that is actually used?

667. Will there be an increase in the political conservatism?

668. How do you maximize short-term return on investment?

669. How is the risk management process used in practice?

670. What is the past performance of the Device Onboarding project manager?

671. Is a software Device Onboarding project management tool available?

672. Assumptions analysis -what assumptions have you made or been given about your Device Onboarding project?

673. How is risk handled within this Device Onboarding project organization?

674. What are the industrial relations prevailing in your organization?

675. How carefully have the potential competitors been identified?

676. Are there alternative opinions/solutions/ processes you should explore?

677. What will be the likely political situation during the life of the Device Onboarding project?

678. Have you worked with the customer in the past?

679. What will be cost of redeployment of personnel?

2.34 Probability and Impact Matrix: Device Onboarding

680. Were there any Device Onboarding projects similar to this one in existence?

681. Which role do you have in the Device Onboarding project?

682. Are formal technical reviews part of this process?

683. How do you define a risk?

684. How are risks and risk management perceived in the Device Onboarding project?

685. What are the probable external agencies to act as Device Onboarding project manager?

686. Which phase of the Device Onboarding project do you take part in?

687. Does the Device Onboarding project team have experience with the technology to be implemented?

688. How solid is the Device Onboarding projection of competitive reaction?

689. Do you have specific methods that you use for each phase of the process?

690. Do the people have the right combinations of skills?

691. Is there any sign of biased ranking?

692. Which should be probably done NEXT?

693. What lifestyle shifts might occur in society?

694. Mandated delivery date?

695. While preparing your risk responses, you identify additional risks. What should you do?

696. Do end-users have realistic expectations?

697. How should you structure risks?

698. How well is the risk understood?

2.35 Risk Data Sheet: Device Onboarding

699. Is the data sufficiently specified in terms of the type of failure being analyzed, and its frequency or probability?

700. Potential for recurrence?

701. What can happen?

702. Do effective diagnostic tests exist?

703. What will be the consequences if it happens?

704. How do you handle product safely?

705. If it happens, what are the consequences?

706. What can you do?

707. Type of risk identified?

708. During work activities could hazards exist?

709. What is the chance that it will happen?

710. What were the Causes that contributed?

711. Are new hazards created?

712. What are you here for (Mission)?

713. Whom do you serve (customers)?

714. How reliable is the data source?

715. What was measured?

716. What are you weak at and therefore need to do better?

2.36 Procurement Management Plan: Device Onboarding

717. Public engagement – did you get it right?

718. Are meeting minutes captured and sent out after meetings?

719. Why is procurement planning important?

720. Are schedule deliverables actually delivered?

721. Alignment to strategic goals & objectives?

722. Are risk oriented checklists used during risk identification?

723. What is the last item a Device Onboarding project manager must do to finalize Device Onboarding project close-out?

724. What are you trying to accomplish?

725. Are decisions captured in a decisions log?

726. Is there a procurement management plan in place?

727. Has a quality assurance plan been developed for the Device Onboarding project?

728. Does the schedule include Device Onboarding project management time and change request

analysis time?

729. Are the people assigned to the Device Onboarding project sufficiently qualified?

730. How will multiple providers be managed?

731. Financial capacity; does the seller have, or can the seller reasonably be expected to obtain, the financial resources needed?

2.37 Source Selection Criteria: Device Onboarding

732. What is cost analysis and when should it be performed?

733. What are the requirements for publicizing a RFP?

734. How important is cost in the source selection decision relative to past performance and technical considerations?

735. What should preproposal conferences accomplish?

736. Who is entitled to a debriefing?

737. When and what information can be considered with offerors regarding past performance?

738. Can you identify proposed teaming partners and/or subcontractors and consider the nature and extent of proposed involvement in satisfying the Device Onboarding project requirements?

739. Is a cost realism analysis used?

740. What should be considered when developing evaluation standards?

741. What information may not be provided?

742. Have all evaluators been trained?

743. Do proposed hours support content and schedule?

744. Who must be notified?

745. How is past performance evaluated?

746. Do you prepare an independent cost estimate?

747. Are evaluators ready to begin this task?

748. With the rapid changes in information technology, will media be readable in five or ten years?

749. Is there collaboration among your evaluators?

750. Are they compliant with all technical requirements?

2.38 Stakeholder Management Plan: Device Onboarding

751. Are there processes in place to ensure internal consistency between the source code components?

752. Is there an on-going process in place to monitor Device Onboarding project risks?

753. When would you develop a Device Onboarding project Business Plan?

754. Are Device Onboarding project contact logs kept up to date?

755. Has a resource management plan been created?

756. Is there an onboarding process in place?

757. Are communication systems currently in place appropriate?

758. What has to be purchased?

759. Is there general agreement & acceptance of the current status and progress of the Device Onboarding project?

760. Do all stakeholders know how to access this repository and where to find the Device Onboarding project documentation?

761. Has a capability assessment been conducted?

762. What proven methodologies and standards will be used to ensure that materials, products, processes and services are fit for purpose?

763. Were Device Onboarding project team members involved in detailed estimating and scheduling?

764. Is staff trained on the software technologies that are being used on the Device Onboarding project?

765. Describe the process that will be used to design, develop, review, accept, distribute and change outputs. Will all outputs delivered by the Device Onboarding project follow the same process?

766. Why is it important to reduce deliverables to a smallest component?

2.39 Change Management Plan: Device Onboarding

767. Why would a Device Onboarding project run more smoothly when change management is emphasized from the beginning?

768. What new competencies will be required for the roles?

769. How will the stakeholders share information and transfer knowledge?

770. Who will be the change levers?

771. Would you need to tailor a special message for each segment of the audience?

772. Has the relevant business unit been notified of installation and support requirements?

773. Who is the audience for change management activities?

774. What relationships will change?

775. How will you deal with anger about the restricting of communications due to confidentiality considerations?

776. Do there need to be new channels developed?

777. Do you need new systems?

778. Has the training provider been established?

779. What do you expect the target audience to do, say, think or feel as a result of this communication?

780. Where will the funds come from?

781. Are work location changes required?

782. What roles within your organization are affected, and how?

783. Readiness -what is a successful end state?

784. What are the responsibilities assigned to each role?

785. Change invariability confront many relationships especially the already stated that require a set of behaviours What roles with in your organization are affected and how?

3.0 Executing Process Group: Device Onboarding

786. What are deliverables of your Device Onboarding project?

787. Who will be the main sponsor?

788. What is the shortest possible time it will take to complete this Device Onboarding project?

789. Based on your Device Onboarding project communication management plan, what worked well?

790. How could you control progress of your Device Onboarding project?

791. Who are the Device Onboarding project stakeholders?

792. Would you rate yourself as being risk-averse, risk-neutral, or risk-seeking?

793. What Device Onboarding projects and services are in the portfolio of your organization?

794. What is the difference between using brainstorming and the Delphi technique for risk identification?

795. Who will provide training?

796. What are crucial elements of successful Device Onboarding project plan execution?

797. What were things that you did very well and want to do the same again on the next Device Onboarding project?

798. What are the Device Onboarding project management deliverables of each process group?

799. What are the typical Device Onboarding project management skills?

800. How well defined and documented were the Device Onboarding project management processes you chose to use?

801. Could a new application negatively affect the current IT infrastructure?

802. Have operating capacities been created and/or reinforced in partners?

3.1 Team Member Status Report: Device Onboarding

803. The problem with Reward & Recognition Programs is that the truly deserving people all too often get left out. How can you make it practical?

804. What is to be done?

805. Why is it to be done?

806. Do you have an Enterprise Device Onboarding project Management Office (EPMO)?

807. How does this product, good, or service meet the needs of the Device Onboarding project and your organization as a whole?

808. Are your organizations Device Onboarding projects more successful over time?

809. How will resource planning be done?

810. Is there evidence that staff is taking a more professional approach toward management of your organizations Device Onboarding projects?

811. Does your organization have the means (staff, money, contract, etc.) to produce or to acquire the product, good, or service?

812. Does every department have to have a Device Onboarding project Manager on staff?

813. Will the staff do training or is that done by a third party?

814. How it is to be done?

815. How can you make it practical?

816. Does the product, good, or service already exist within your organization?

817. What specific interest groups do you have in place?

818. Are the products of your organizations Device Onboarding projects meeting customers objectives?

819. Are the attitudes of staff regarding Device Onboarding project work improving?

820. When a teams productivity and success depend on collaboration and the efficient flow of information, what generally fails them?

821. How much risk is involved?

3.2 Change Request: Device Onboarding

822. What is the function of the change control committee?

823. What are the duties of the change control team?

824. How can you ensure that changes have been made properly?

825. Since there are no change requests in your Device Onboarding project at this point, what must you have before you begin?

826. How many times must the change be modified or presented to the change control board before it is approved?

827. What can be filed?

828. Who is included in the change control team?

829. What must be taken into consideration when introducing change control programs?

830. Will the change use memory to the extent that other functions will be not have sufficient memory to operate effectively?

831. What are the requirements for urgent changes?

832. How do team members communicate with each

other?

833. Who is communicating the change?

834. Why do you want to have a change control system?

835. Who is responsible for the implementation and monitoring of all measures?

836. Who is responsible to authorize changes?

837. Will there be a change request form in use?

838. How does a team identify the discrete elements of a configuration?

839. Has a formal technical review been conducted to assess technical correctness?

840. What should be regulated in a change control operating instruction?

841. What are the basic mechanics of the Change Advisory Board (CAB)?

3.3 Change Log: Device Onboarding

842. When was the request approved?

843. Is the change request within Device Onboarding project scope?

844. Is the requested change request a result of changes in other Device Onboarding project(s)?

845. Do the described changes impact on the integrity or security of the system?

846. Is the submitted change a new change or a modification of a previously approved change?

847. How does this change affect scope?

848. How does this relate to the standards developed for specific business processes?

849. Is the change request open, closed or pending?

850. Will the Device Onboarding project fail if the change request is not executed?

851. When was the request submitted?

852. Is this a mandatory replacement?

853. Where do changes come from?

854. How does this change affect the timeline of the schedule?

855. Who initiated the change request?

856. Does the suggested change request seem to represent a necessary enhancement to the product?

857. Does the suggested change request represent a desired enhancement to the products functionality?

858. Should a more thorough impact analysis be conducted?

859. Is the change backward compatible without limitations?

3.4 Decision Log: Device Onboarding

860. Does anything need to be adjusted?

861. How does the use a Decision Support System influence the strategies/tactics or costs?

862. How consolidated and comprehensive a story can you tell by capturing currently available incident data in a central location and through a log of key decisions during an incident?

863. What was the rationale for the decision?

864. What eDiscovery problem or issue did your organization set out to fix or make better?

865. Decision-making process; how will the team make decisions?

866. With whom was the decision shared or considered?

867. Linked to original objective?

868. Behaviors; what are guidelines that the team has identified that will assist them with getting the most out of team meetings?

869. It becomes critical to track and periodically revisit both operational effectiveness; Are you noticing all that you need to, and are you interpreting what you see effectively?

870. How do you define success?

871. Is everything working as expected?

872. Do strategies and tactics aimed at less than full control reduce the costs of management or simply shift the cost burden?

873. Adversarial environment. is your opponent open to a non-traditional workflow, or will it likely challenge anything you do?

874. What is the line where eDiscovery ends and document review begins?

875. Who is the decisionmaker?

876. How does provision of information, both in terms of content and presentation, influence acceptance of alternative strategies?

877. Who will be given a copy of this document and where will it be kept?

878. What is your overall strategy for quality control / quality assurance procedures?

879. What makes you different or better than others companies selling the same thing?

3.5 Quality Audit: Device Onboarding

880. How does your organization know that its range of activities are being reviewed as rigorously and constructively as they could be?

881. How does your organization know that its promotions system is appropriately effective, constructive and fair?

882. How does your organization know that it is effectively and constructively guiding staff through to timely completion of tasks?

883. Is progress against the intentions measurable?

884. Is your organizational structure a help or a hindrance to deployment?

885. Is quality audit a prerequisite for program accreditation or program recognition?

886. Are goals well supported with strategies, operational plans, manuals and training?

887. How does your organization know that the range and quality of its accommodation, catering and transportation services are appropriately effective and constructive?

888. Has a written procedure been established to identify devices during all stages of receipt, reconditioning, distribution and installation so that mix-ups are prevented?

889. What is the collective experience of the team to be assigned to an audit?

890. Is the reports overall tone appropriate?

891. How does your organization know that the review processes are effective?

892. How is the Strategic Plan (and other plans) reviewed and revised?

893. How does your organization know that its staff embody the core knowledge, skills and characteristics for which it wishes to be recognized?

894. How does your organization know that its relationship with its (past) staff is appropriately effective and constructive?

895. How does your organization know that its system for examining work done is appropriately effective and constructive?

896. How well do you think your organization engages with the outside community?

897. How does your organization know that its quality of teaching is appropriately effective and constructive?

898. How does your organization know that its systems for meeting staff extracurricular learning support requirements are appropriately effective and constructive?

899. Are the intentions consistent with external obligations (such as applicable laws)?

3.6 Team Directory: Device Onboarding

900. How will the team handle changes?

901. How will you accomplish and manage the objectives?

902. Where will the product be used and/or delivered or built when appropriate?

903. Who are your stakeholders (customers, sponsors, end users, team members)?

904. Process decisions: do job conditions warrant additional actions to collect job information and document on-site activity?

905. Process decisions: do invoice amounts match accepted work in place?

906. Where should the information be distributed?

907. When will you produce deliverables?

908. How and in what format should information be presented?

909. Process decisions: are contractors adequately prosecuting the work?

910. Who will be the stakeholders on your next Device Onboarding project?

911. Process decisions: how well was task order work performed?

912. Days from the time the issue is identified?

913. What needs to be communicated?

914. When does information need to be distributed?

915. Contract requirements complied with?

916. Who are the Team Members?

917. Process decisions: are all start-up, turn over and close out requirements of the contract satisfied?

3.7 Team Operating Agreement: Device Onboarding

918. What are some potential sources of conflict among team members?

919. What resources can be provided for the team in terms of equipment, space, time for training, protected time and space for meetings, and travel allowances?

920. What is your unique contribution to your organization?

921. Do you leverage technology engagement tools group chat, polls, screen sharing, etc.?

922. Are there more than two national cultures represented by your team?

923. Did you prepare participants for the next meeting?

924. Do you ensure that all participants know how to use the required technology?

925. What types of accommodations will be formulated and put in place for sustaining the team?

926. Are there more than two functional areas represented by your team?

927. How do you want to be thought of and known

within your organization?

928. Did you delegate tasks such as taking meeting minutes, presenting a topic and soliciting input?

929. Must your members collaborate successfully to complete Device Onboarding projects?

930. Do you brief absent members after they view meeting notes or listen to a recording?

931. Are there differences in access to communication and collaboration technology based on team member location?

932. Confidentiality: how will confidential information be handled?

933. How will your group handle planned absences?

934. Does your team need access to all documents and information at all times?

935. What is group supervision?

936. Is compensation based on team and individual performance?

3.8 Team Performance Assessment: Device Onboarding

937. What are you doing specifically to develop the leaders around you?

938. Delaying market entry: how long is too long?

939. To what degree will team members, individually and collectively, commit time to help themselves and others learn and develop skills?

940. How much interpersonal friction is there in your team?

941. Do you give group members authority to make at least some important decisions?

942. To what degree can the team measure progress against specific goals?

943. To what degree are the goals realistic?

944. Can team performance be reliably measured in simulator and live exercises using the same assessment tool?

945. How does Device Onboarding project termination impact Device Onboarding project team members?

946. To what degree does the teams approach to its work allow for modification and improvement over

time?

947. To what degree are the relative importance and priority of the goals clear to all team members?

948. How do you encourage members to learn from each other?

949. Social categorization and intergroup behaviour: Does minimal intergroup discrimination make social identity more positive?

950. To what degree does the team possess adequate membership to achieve its ends?

951. How do you keep key people outside the group informed about its accomplishments?

952. To what degree does the teams work approach provide opportunity for members to engage in results-based evaluation?

953. To what degree does the teams work approach provide opportunity for members to engage in open interaction?

954. Lack of method variance in self-reported affect and perceptions at work: Reality or artifact?

955. To what degree are the goals ambitious?

956. If you are worried about method variance before you collect data, what sort of design elements might you include to reduce or eliminate the threat of method variance?

3.9 Team Member Performance Assessment: Device Onboarding

957. What are top priorities?

958. What is the large, desired outcome?

959. What is the target group for instruction (e.g., individual and collective or small team instruction)?

960. How should adaptive assessments be implemented?

961. How do you determine which data are the most important to use, analyze, or review?

962. How are assessments designed, delivered, and otherwise used to maximize training?

963. What makes them effective?

964. Are any validation activities performed?

965. What instructional strategies were developed/ incorporated (e.g., direct instruction, indirect instruction, experiential learning, independent study, interactive instruction)?

966. What specific plans do you have for developing effective cross-platform assessments in a blended learning environment?

967. How do you make use of research?

968. How is assessment information achieved, stored?

969. What are they responsible for?

970. How was the determination made for which training platforms would be used (i.e., media selection)?

971. To what degree are the skill areas critical to team performance present?

972. For what period of time is a member rated?

973. What, if any, steps are available for employees who feel they have been unfairly or inaccurately rated?

974. What changes do you need to make to align practices with beliefs?

975. How is your organizations Strategic Management System tied to performance measurement?

3.10 Issue Log: Device Onboarding

976. How do you manage human resources?

977. What date was the issue resolved?

978. Who do you turn to if you have questions?

979. Are they needed?

980. Persistence; will users learn a work around or will they be bothered every time?

981. What is the impact on the Business Case?

982. Where do team members get information?

983. Which stakeholders are thought leaders, influences, or early adopters?

984. What is a Stakeholder?

985. What is the status of the issue?

986. What approaches to you feel are the best ones to use?

987. What would have to change?

988. Who reported the issue?

989. Why not more evaluators?

990. What effort will a change need?

991. How is this initiative related to other portfolios, programs, or Device Onboarding projects?

992. How do you reply to this question; you am new here and managing this major program. How do you suggest you build your network?

993. Are the Device Onboarding project issues uniquely identified, including to which product they refer?

994. Which team member will work with each stakeholder?

4.0 Monitoring and Controlling Process Group: Device Onboarding

995. Feasibility: how much money, time, and effort can you put into this?

996. Does the solution fit in with organizations technical architectural requirements?

997. How will staff learn how to use the deliverables?

998. Is the verbiage used appropriate and understandable?

999. Is there sufficient time allotted between the general system design and the detailed system design phases?

1000. What factors are contributing to progress or delay in the achievement of products and results?

1001. How is agile portfolio management done?

1002. Mitigate. what will you do to minimize the impact should a risk event occur?

1003. What were things that you need to improve?

1004. Did you implement the program as designed?

1005. Is it what was agreed upon?

1006. What communication items need

improvement?

1007. What were things that you did well, and could improve, and how?

1008. Propriety: who needs to be involved in the evaluation to be ethical?

1009. Is the program making progress in helping to achieve the set results?

1010. Is there sufficient funding available for this?

1011. Is progress on outcomes due to your program?

4.1 Project Performance Report: Device Onboarding

1012. What is the degree to which rules govern information exchange between individuals within your organization?

1013. To what degree are the tasks requirements reflected in the flow and storage of information?

1014. To what degree does the task meet individual needs?

1015. To what degree do team members agree with the goals, relative importance, and the ways in which achievement will be measured?

1016. How will procurement be coordinated with other Device Onboarding project aspects, such as scheduling and performance reporting?

1017. To what degree do the goals specify concrete team work products?

1018. What is the degree to which rules govern information exchange between groups?

1019. To what degree are the demands of the task compatible with and converge with the relationships of the informal organization?

1020. To what degree can team members meet frequently enough to accomplish the teams ends?

1021. To what degree is the information network consistent with the structure of the formal organization?

1022. To what degree do individual skills and abilities match task demands?

1023. To what degree are fresh input and perspectives systematically caught and added (for example, through information and analysis, new members, and senior sponsors)?

1024. To what degree do team members feel that the purpose of the team is important, if not exciting?

1025. Next Steps?

1026. How is the data used?

1027. To what degree are the structures of the formal organization consistent with the behaviors in the informal organization?

1028. To what degree can team members vigorously define the teams purpose in considerations with others who are not part of the functioning team?

1029. To what degree can the cognitive capacity of individuals accommodate the flow of information?

1030. To what degree will new and supplemental skills be introduced as the need is recognized?

4.2 Variance Analysis: Device Onboarding

1031. Are there changes in the direct base to which overhead costs are allocated?

1032. What is your organizations rationale for sharing expenses and services between business segments?

1033. Are your organizations and items of cost assigned to each pool identified?

1034. Is the anticipated (firm and potential) business base Device Onboarding projected in a rational, consistent manner?

1035. Are there knowledgeable Device Onboarding projections of future performance?

1036. What is the incurrence of actual indirect costs in excess of budgets, by element of expense?

1037. At what point should variances be isolated and brought to the attention of the management?

1038. Are overhead cost budgets established for each department which has authority to incur overhead costs?

1039. Is work properly classified as measured effort, LOE, or apportioned effort and appropriately separated?

1040. How do you manage changes in the nature of the overhead requirements?

1041. Are there changes in the overhead pool and/or organization structures?

1042. What can be the cause of an increase in costs?

1043. The anticipated business volume?

1044. How does the monthly budget compare to the actual experience?

1045. Can process improvements lead to unfavorable variances?

1046. How does your organization allocate the cost of shared expenses and services?

4.3 Earned Value Status: Device Onboarding

1047. Where are your problem areas?

1048. Are you hitting your Device Onboarding projects targets?

1049. Verification is a process of ensuring that the developed system satisfies the stakeholders agreements and specifications; Are you building the product right? What do you verify?

1050. If earned value management (EVM) is so good in determining the true status of a Device Onboarding project and Device Onboarding project its completion, why is it that hardly any one uses it in information systems related Device Onboarding projects?

1051. Where is evidence-based earned value in your organization reported?

1052. Earned value can be used in almost any Device Onboarding project situation and in almost any Device Onboarding project environment. it may be used on large Device Onboarding projects, medium sized Device Onboarding projects, tiny Device Onboarding projects (in cut-down form), complex and simple Device Onboarding projects and in any market sector. some people, of course, know all about earned value, they have used it for years - but perhaps not as effectively as they could have?

1053. What is the unit of forecast value?

1054. When is it going to finish?

1055. How much is it going to cost by the finish?

1056. How does this compare with other Device Onboarding projects?

1057. Validation is a process of ensuring that the developed system will actually achieve the stakeholders desired outcomes; Are you building the right product? What do you validate?

4.4 Risk Audit: Device Onboarding

1058. What is the implication of budget constraint on this process?

1059. Have risks been considered with an insurance broker or provider and suitable insurance cover been arranged?

1060. Are tool mentors available?

1061. Does your auditor understand your business?

1062. Risks with Device Onboarding projects or new initiatives?

1063. Do you have an understanding of insurance claims processes?

1064. Are audit program plans risk-adjusted?

1065. Does your organization meet the terms of any contracts with which it is involved?

1066. Are duties out-of-class?

1067. Can assurance be expanded beyond the traditional audit without undermining independence?

1068. Do you have position descriptions for all office bearers/staff?

1069. What are the commonly used work arounds in high risk areas?

1070. Does your organization communicate regularly and effectively with its members?

1071. Are you aware of the industry standards that apply to your operations?

1072. What expertise does the Board have on quality, outcomes, and errors?

1073. Does the customer have a solid idea of what is required?

1074. How effective are your risk controls?

1075. Are policies communicated to all affected?

1076. Are you meeting your legal, regulatory and compliance requirements - if not, why not?

4.5 Contractor Status Report: Device Onboarding

1077. What was the actual budget or estimated cost for your organizations services?

1078. What was the overall budget or estimated cost?

1079. How long have you been using the services?

1080. If applicable; describe your standard schedule for new software version releases. Are new software version releases included in the standard maintenance plan?

1081. What are the minimum and optimal bandwidth requirements for the proposed solution?

1082. Who can list a Device Onboarding project as organization experience, your organization or a previous employee of your organization?

1083. Are there contractual transfer concerns?

1084. What was the budget or estimated cost for your organizations services?

1085. How is risk transferred?

1086. Describe how often regular updates are made to the proposed solution. Are corresponding regular updates included in the standard maintenance plan?

1087. What was the final actual cost?

1088. What process manages the contracts?

1089. What is the average response time for answering a support call?

4.6 Formal Acceptance: Device Onboarding

1090. Does it do what Device Onboarding project team said it would?

1091. How does your team plan to obtain formal acceptance on your Device Onboarding project?

1092. What function(s) does it fill or meet?

1093. Is formal acceptance of the Device Onboarding project product documented and distributed?

1094. Was the client satisfied with the Device Onboarding project results?

1095. Do you buy-in installation services?

1096. Did the Device Onboarding project manager and team act in a professional and ethical manner?

1097. How well did the team follow the methodology?

1098. Who would use it?

1099. Was the Device Onboarding project managed well?

1100. Was the Device Onboarding project work done on time, within budget, and according to specification?

1101. Was business value realized?

1102. Did the Device Onboarding project achieve its MOV?

1103. Do you perform formal acceptance or burn-in tests?

1104. Who supplies data?

1105. What can you do better next time?

1106. What are the requirements against which to test, Who will execute?

1107. Does it do what client said it would?

1108. What was done right?

1109. What is the Acceptance Management Process?

5.0 Closing Process Group: Device Onboarding

1110. How dependent is the Device Onboarding project on other Device Onboarding projects or work efforts?

1111. Did you do what you said you were going to do?

1112. What is the Device Onboarding project Management Process?

1113. How critical is the Device Onboarding project success to the success of your organization?

1114. What were the desired outcomes?

1115. Is there a clear cause and effect between the activity and the lesson learned?

1116. If a risk event occurs, what will you do?

1117. Just how important is your work to the overall success of the Device Onboarding project?

1118. What level of risk does the proposed budget represent to the Device Onboarding project?

1119. What is the risk of failure to your organization?

1120. Is the Device Onboarding project funded?

1121. Is this a follow-on to a previous Device

Onboarding project?

1122. What is the Device Onboarding project name and date of completion?

1123. Was the user/client satisfied with the end product?

1124. Specific - is the objective clear in terms of what, how, when, and where the situation will be changed?

1125. What was learned?

5.1 Procurement Audit: Device Onboarding

1126. Does the department have a procurement strategy and is it implemented?

1127. Are known obligations, such as salaries and contracts, encumbered at the beginning of the year?

1128. Are information technology resources (e-procurement) used to reduce costs?

1129. Was invitation to tender to each specific contract issued after the evaluation of the indicative tenders was completed?

1130. Did your organization permit tenderers to submit variants, thus offering space for creative solutions and added value?

1131. Did the contracting authority offer unrestricted and full electronic access to the contract documents and any supplementary documents (specifying the internet address in the notice)?

1132. Are review meetings organized during contract execution and do they meet demand?

1133. Are there appropriate controls in place to ensure that procurement complies with the relevant legislation?

1134. Did your organization identify the full contract

value and include options and provisions for renewals?

1135. When competitive dialogue was used, did the contracting authority provide sufficient justification for the use of this procedure and was the contract actually particularly complex?

1136. Are outsourcing and Public Private Partnerships considered as alternatives to in-house work?

1137. Were there no material changes in the contract shortly after award?

1138. Does your organization maintain a current file of vendors and vendor catalogues?

1139. Must the receipt of goods be approved prior to payment?

1140. Is the functioning of automatic disbursement programs tested by an independent party?

1141. Are advantages and disadvantages of in-house production, outsourcing and Public Private Partnerships considered?

1142. Are all purchase orders cancelled after payment to avoid duplicate payment of the same invoice?

1143. Are reports based on sound data available to the already stated responsible for monitoring the performance of contracts?

1144. Is the performance of the procurement function/unit regularly evaluated?

1145. Is the opportunity properly published?

5.2 Contract Close-Out: Device Onboarding

1146. Are the signers the authorized officials?

1147. Have all contracts been completed?

1148. Have all contract records been included in the Device Onboarding project archives?

1149. Change in knowledge?

1150. Has each contract been audited to verify acceptance and delivery?

1151. Was the contract type appropriate?

1152. Change in attitude or behavior?

1153. Was the contract sufficiently clear so as not to result in numerous disputes and misunderstandings?

1154. Have all acceptance criteria been met prior to final payment to contractors?

1155. Why Outsource?

1156. How does it work?

1157. Have all contracts been closed?

1158. Change in circumstances?

1159. What happens to the recipient of services?

1160. What is capture management?

1161. Parties: who is involved?

1162. How/when used ?

1163. How is the contracting office notified of the automatic contract close-out?

1164. Was the contract complete without requiring numerous changes and revisions?

1165. Parties: Authorized?

5.3 Project or Phase Close-Out: Device Onboarding

1166. What information is each stakeholder group interested in?

1167. Who is responsible for award close-out?

1168. Have business partners been involved extensively, and what data was required for them?

1169. Were the outcomes different from the already stated planned?

1170. Did the Device Onboarding project management methodology work?

1171. Were messages directly related to the release strategy or phases of the Device Onboarding project?

1172. Did the delivered product meet the specified requirements and goals of the Device Onboarding project?

1173. Which changes might a stakeholder be required to make as a result of the Device Onboarding project?

1174. What stakeholder group needs, expectations, and interests are being met by the Device Onboarding project?

1175. How often did each stakeholder need an update?

1176. Who are the Device Onboarding project stakeholders and what are roles and involvement?

1177. What are the marketing communication needs for each stakeholder?

1178. What hierarchical authority does the stakeholder have in your organization?

1179. What were the goals and objectives of the communications strategy for the Device Onboarding project?

1180. Planned remaining costs?

1181. Planned completion date?

5.4 Lessons Learned: Device Onboarding

1182. How effectively were issues resolved before escalation was necessary?

1183. How extensive is middle management?

1184. How does the budget cycle affect the case?

1185. Were the right people available when required?

1186. How adaptable is the deliverable?

1187. Who had fiscal authority to manage the funding for the Device Onboarding project, did that work?

1188. Were any objectives unmet?

1189. What if anything has been lacking?

1190. What would you change?

1191. Did the team work well together?

1192. How effective were your functional specs?

1193. Was any formal risk assessment carried out at the start of the Device Onboarding project, and was this followed up during the Device Onboarding project?

1194. What did you put in place to ensure success?

1195. How efficient is the deliverable?

1196. What is your organizations performance history?

1197. How accurately and timely was the Risk Management Log updated or reviewed?

1198. How many government and contractor personnel are authorized for the Device Onboarding project?

1199. How effective was the acceptance management process?

Index

ignore 17
ignoring   117
imbedded   90
impact 4, 36, 45, 51, 53, 84, 132, 142, 181, 197, 199, 201, 203,
221-222, 232, 236, 238
impacted   55, 128, 148
impacts   48, 199
implement   21, 47, 71, 88, 189, 238
implicit 102
importance   233, 240
important   16-17, 33, 59, 68, 102-103, 106, 111, 114, 170, 185,
196, 207, 209, 212, 232, 234, 241, 252
improve   2, 9, 65, 73-75, 78-80, 82, 87, 238-239
improved   73, 78-79, 99
improving   218
incentives   95
incident   223
include   25, 82, 84, 153, 207, 233, 255
included   2, 7, 18, 149, 171, 179, 219, 248, 257
INCLUDES   9
including   16, 35, 37, 43, 52, 64, 90, 92, 94, 156, 237
increase   75, 111, 149, 201, 243
increased   118
increasing   123
incurred   44
incurrence   242
in-depth   8, 10
indicate   59, 92, 108
indicated   99
indicative   254
indicators   23, 48, 53, 59, 61, 71, 80, 90, 190
indirect   48, 152, 178, 234, 242
indirectly   1
individual   1, 46, 128, 171, 193, 231, 234, 240-241
industrial   202
industry   98, 104, 122, 162, 247
infinite 114
influence   108, 128, 131, 134, 192, 196, 223-224
influences   236
informal   240-241
informed   120, 233
ingrained   91
inherent   115

limited 9, 192
linked 36, 143, 223
listed   1
listen   117, 122, 231
locally 175
located   175
location   214, 223, 231
logical 165
longer 93
long-term   97, 104, 110
Looking   18
losses   24, 30
magnitude   83
maintain   88, 115-116, 255
maintained   169
makers 97, 127, 177
making   17, 66, 77, 84, 104, 187, 239
manage   30, 37, 43, 49, 52, 65, 71, 79-80, 111, 118, 136,
144, 159, 177, 199, 228, 236, 243, 261
manageable 35, 81
managed   7, 33, 58, 65, 68, 80-81, 84-85, 90, 97, 208, 250
management 1, 3-5, 8-9, 16, 21, 26, 37, 51, 60, 63-65, 67-68, 75,
78, 81, 105-106, 118, 124, 134, 136, 138, 140, 146-149, 152, 155-
156, 159, 168, 175, 177, 181-183, 187, 189, 193, 195, 197, 200-203,
207, 211, 213, 215-217, 224, 235, 238, 242, 244, 251-252, 258-259,
261-262
manager   7, 9, 17, 29, 116, 170, 183, 202-203, 207, 217, 250
managers   2, 126, 137, 153, 169
manages   76, 81, 129, 249
managing   2, 76, 126, 131, 237
Mandated   204
mandatory   221
manner   24, 85, 127, 139, 152-153, 242, 250
manpower   193
mantle 107
manuals   225
Mapping   60, 65, 70
market 26, 162, 198, 232, 244
marketable   198
marketer   7
Marketing   103, 133, 260
markets   21
material   153, 161, 255

prevents   17
previous   29, 174, 248, 252
previously   221
priced 152
primary   44
principles   134
priorities   43-44, 50-51, 234
prioritize   189, 201
priority 48-49, 233
privacy   37, 185
Private 255
probable   203
probably   204
problem   15-19, 21-22, 27, 29, 38, 42, 47, 61-62, 217, 223,
244
problems   16, 19, 21-23, 25, 75, 83-84, 99, 110, 133, 135, 142,
188
procedure   225, 255
procedures   9, 76, 90-91, 95-96, 138, 152, 155, 165, 169, 177,
183, 188, 193, 224
proceed   152
proceeding   194
process   1-7, 9, 27-28, 31, 35, 39, 41, 52, 58-71, 74, 86, 89-
93, 95-99, 127-128, 134, 136, 138-139, 142-144, 146-149, 156, 165,
170, 172, 183, 187, 193, 197-198, 200-201, 203, 211-212, 215-216,
223, 228-229, 238, 243-246, 249, 251-252, 262
processes   58-59, 61, 63-65, 67, 69-71, 88, 92, 95, 127-128,
148, 169, 184, 197, 202, 211-212, 216, 221, 226, 246
produce   65, 127, 165, 217, 228
produced   66, 85
producing   144, 147
product   1, 47, 59, 118, 161-162, 181-182, 185, 197-198,
205, 217-218, 222, 228, 237, 244-245, 250, 253, 259
production   35, 81, 118, 255
products   1, 16, 25, 110, 117, 129, 141, 144, 178, 212, 218,
222, 238, 240
profits 181
program   17, 48, 90, 134, 137, 184, 225, 237-239, 246
programs   217, 219, 237, 255
progress   32, 55, 94, 104, 119, 128, 134, 155, 179, 183, 187,
211, 215, 225, 232, 238-239

repeatable   201
rephrased   9
replace   43
Report 5-6, 74, 97, 139, 161, 217, 240, 248
reported   185, 236, 244
reporting   63, 91, 124, 140-141, 156, 185, 190, 197, 240
reports 55, 92, 131, 137, 139, 141, 190, 226, 255
repository   211
represent   79, 222, 252
reproduced   1
reputation   111
request   5, 62, 182, 207, 219-222
requested   1, 84, 127, 221
requests   219
require 29, 45, 58, 71, 88, 99, 152, 165, 199, 214
required   16, 25, 30, 33, 35, 37, 39, 46, 63, 71, 74, 77, 86, 98,
158-159, 171, 185, 213-214, 230, 247, 259, 261
requiring   131, 258
research   26, 102, 118, 234
Reserve   152, 177
reserved   1
reside 83
resolution   62, 85
resolve 16, 25
resolved   139, 197, 236, 261
resource   3-4, 121, 135, 152, 160, 165, 167, 176, 193, 211,
217
resources   2, 7, 17, 21-22, 36-37, 54, 86, 98, 101, 114, 121,
127, 129, 132, 146, 149, 156, 158-159, 163, 167, 180, 208, 230,
236, 254
respect   1
respond   135, 199
responded   11
response   17, 26, 89-90, 92-93, 99, 249
responses   120, 204
responsive   171, 180
restrict 142
result   63, 79, 85, 153, 177, 180, 183, 195, 214, 221, 257, 259
resulted   94
resulting   70, 137
results 8, 28, 32, 73-78, 80, 82, 86, 90, 95, 127, 134, 160, 170, 179,
189, 238-239, 250
Retain 101